Handley Page O/400 Night Bomber Pilot - "A Brave Aviator and a Gentleman"

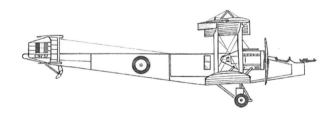

The World War I Operational Service of 2nd Lieutenant
A.C.G. (Garrie) Fowler, RAF, No. 215 Squadron
Killed in Action 20 September, 1918

Handley Page O/400 Night Bomber Pilot - "A Brave Aviator and a Gentleman"

A Short History

By

C.G. and P.V. Hunt

This edition published 2018

Front cover: From an original painting titled, *"In Roaring They Shall Rise..."* by Neil Hipkiss GAvA, © Neil Hipkiss, used with permission.

Back cover: Crests - Public Domain; Memorial Plaque – by A. Gillatt, used with permission.

Disclaimer: The views, thoughts, and opinions expressed in the text belong solely to the authors, and while we have taken every precaution to ensure that the content of this book is accurate, errors can occur. Some of the events that relate solely to the final flight of 2nd Lieutenant A.C.G. Fowler and crew on 20 September, 1918 are necessarily an attempt to piece together from the facts available what actually occurred that night in the air but with no surviving eyewitness, they are at best, a reasonably informed commentary and an epitaph to brave aircrew. Invariably, we have attempted to employ historical evidence, often drawing on actual opinions expressed contemporaneously during the period of World War I and shortly, after. We assume no responsibility or liability for any errors or omissions in the content of this book and the information contained within is provided on an "as is" basis with no guarantees of completeness, accuracy and usefulness. It is simply an effort to commemorate a long dead relation and to give context to how and why his sacrifice was made.

ISBN 978-1-7321883-0-3

Printed in the USA by Gasch Printing, LLC, Odenton, Maryland, USA

Contents

List of Figures

Commemoration

For Great Uncle Garrie

World War I Memorial Death Plaque for Alfred Charles Garrett Fowler,
issued after the end of hostilities to the next-of-kin of all British and Empire
service personnel who were killed as a result of the war

Acknowledgments

Heartfelt thanks to family, friends and institutions:

To family: the interest was sparked by my parents starting the quest to find out about the exploits of 2/Lt ACG Fowler. So this writing is carried out in memory of Margaret and Harold Gillatt and their earlier research; also, many thanks to my sister, Anne, for completing a large amount of the background research, including adding to the richness of knowledge about other squadron members. To Chris and Joy Hunt for answering lots of general World War One questions and their quest for commemorating the WWI fallen in London.

To friends including Toni and Ray Fow - with Ray, now sadly having passed, I was able to experience flight in an open-cockpit biplane. I am extraordinarily fortunate to have experienced this.

To friends for reviewing early drafts for aviation sense - Commander Steve George RN, Commander Soapy Watson RN and Captain Earl Smith USN; also, in recognition of other friends who listened to our interminable stories and whose encouragement was unflagging.

To institutions such as the National Archives who give access to the public to precious historical material and carefully guard their charge of this amazing collection for future generations of "sleuths". How so much WWI material survived the transition from war to peace and through the next one hundred years is almost unbelievable.

To the Commonwealth War Graves Commission in our attempt to find Garrie's grave and for memorializing so many who died long before their time.

To the Canada Aviation and Space Museum in Ottawa for helping us find contemporary WWI artifacts from 215 Squadron Canadian pilot Lt. H.B. Monaghan.

To authors and the publishers of books by Garrie's contemporary squadron members: Ray Gentle Communications Ltd., Burlington, Canada (H.B. Monaghan's *Night Bombers of World War One*), Edward Willett (on-line memoirs by his grandfather-in-law, Sampson J. Goodfellow),

Hardpress Publishing, Miami, USA (P. Bewsher's *Green Balls of Fire*). And other authors and publishers who keep adding to the repository of knowledge of WWI history. And including contributors to the Imperial War Museum's Lives of the First World War and to the Merseyside at War website run by Liverpool John Moores University with Jack Lacy's account of his experiences in 215 Squadron. Special appreciation to George K. Williams and his outstanding treatise "Biplanes and Bombsights British Bombing in World War I" which provided insightful and definitive guidance on the background to Independent Force establishment and operations.

To artist Neil Hipkiss, GAvA, whose outstanding oil painting, *"In Roaring They Shall Rise…"* depicts the adrenalin-pumping moment when Handley Page O/400 C9732, making its last low-altitude attack on the enemy Frescaty aerodrome, passes over the grand house, Casino de Frescaty. Neil is an Aviation Artist whose original oil paintings are both authentically dramatic and highly detailed and was first choice to depict the event.

Artist Neil Hipkis, GAvA, at the easel

To the Director of Frescaty-Metz Airfield, France—now a reserve French air base

To The Hertfordshire Express for publishing articles relating to Uncle Garrie.

To the Shuttleworth Collection, Old Warden, Bedfordshire, UK for keeping night bombers of WWI alive with their photographic display—and for having one of the few HP O/400 relics still in existence on display—a fragment of propeller.

To the Royal Air Force Museum, Cosford, UK for storing other parts of HP O/400s—propeller and wing parts.

To Hitchin Grammar School, the East Anglian School and Regent Street Polytechnic for maintaining their WWI rolls of honour.

For Hertfordshire District Council and Hitchin town for maintaining the War Memorial near the town centre.

And last, and most importantly, in memory of the young men of No. 215 Squadron, Royal Air Force; to those that died young in aerial operations and denied the opportunity to grow old and to those that served and then grayed with the passing years but with their memories of shared mission and dangers still intact and sharp, now, nigh on one hundred years past, age no longer wearies even them. But we remember them as:

Fierce fiery warriors fought upon the clouds

In ranks and squadrons and right form of war

The noise of battle hurtled in the air

...And I do fear them

Calpurnia's Dream (Shakespeare's *Julius Caesar*, Act 2, Scene2)

Introduction

The following pages are about one pilot's story of night bombing on the Western Front during the closing stages of World War One

This story is about my great uncle Alfred Charles Garrett Fowler's experiences as a night bomber pilot in 1918. It has been a significant research effort as there were no personal journals and little family folklore.

I never knew my great uncle. He died long before I was born and the family didn't retain pictures of him or his exploits, as far as I know. Researching, I found that I had more common with my great uncle than I could have anticipated, including an interest in Science, in general, and Chemistry in particular. He won the Science prize at his school, the East Anglian School in Bury St. Edmunds and was awarded a distinction in Chemistry in the Cambridge Local Examinations. The connection was that I studied Chemistry at university. However, he left his secondary school to study Electrical Engineering at the Regent Street Polytechnic in London, W.1 and went on to become qualified in Wireless Telegraphy in the Royal Naval Voluntary Reserve, R.N.V.R. at Crystal Palace, London. He then transferred to the Royal Naval Air Service, R.N.A.S. and to pilot training. The R.N.A.S. has been interwoven through my life as well with over a quarter of a century as a Naval Air Service, Fleet Air Arm, spouse. And I have a fraction of Garrie's flying hours under my belt, too, as a pilot of a Cessna 172.

Three months before his death, he celebrated his nineteenth birthday. Nineteen was the official age for participation in combat, although many younger soldiers and sailors responded to the call to arms and fought. He died barely six weeks before the Armistice and the end the Great War after twenty-one night-bombing missions.

The crew of Handley Page O/400 C9732 were three of nearly three-quarters of a million British and almost ten million military personnel killed or missing in action worldwide in World War One.

Uncle Garrie came into our lives when my parents started to research his military history. My Mother was Uncle Garrie's niece. She and my Father started researching his exploits with trips to the National Archives, Kew and viewing the original Operation Orders and Mission Reports. They also visited the East Anglian School in Bury St. Edmunds, which displays their Roll of Honour bearing Uncle Garrie's name. My sister, Garrie's other great niece, has completed significant research into Garrie's military career as well as a number of his fellow squadron comrades including his two fellow crew members on the last, fateful mission - 2/Lt Clement Clough Eaves and 2/Lt John Shannon Ferguson. The life histories she wrote on Garrie's two crew members and that of other members of 215 Squadron including Commanding Officer Maj. J.F. Jones, D.F.C., 2/Lt J.P. Armitage, 2/Lt W.J. Boon, Capt. G.S. Buck, 2/Lt W.J.N. Chalklin, 2/Lt H. Davies, Lt H.R. Dodd, Captain W.B. Lawson, 2/Lt A. Fairhurst, Lt C.C. Fisher, 2/Lt E.C. Jeffkins, 2/Lt R.E. Kestell, Lt H.B. Monaghan, 2/Lt T.V. Preedy, and that of Garrie, 2/Lt A.C.G. Fowler can be seen on the Imperial War Museum's (IWM) website of Lives of the First World War. Also, on Garrie's IWM page is a photograph of the only artifact left from his short life—the Memorial Plaque presented to his next of kin—elder sister Connie, elder brother Bernard and younger sister Christabel.

As a secondary school and high school teacher, many of my Upper Sixth/Senior graduating students were 18. This was Garrie's age as he headed to war—the "war to end all wars"—as the pilot of a behemoth of an aeroplane. The Handley Page O/400 was a biplane with a one hundred-foot wingspan that looked more like a close relative to the Wright Brothers' first airplane than the modern airplanes of today. His medical records noted that Garrie was strikingly tall and lean—6 feet 2 inches tall with a chest measurement of 36 ¾ inches and so, he was considered ideal for piloting the enormous Handley Page O/400 that required long reach and strength. It was barely a decade after the historic first manned, powered flight that the precursor of the HP O/400 became operational. The earlier Handley Page O/100 was intended to deliver the heaviest ordnance load and inflict the most damage on strategic targets of the Central Powers. The HP O/400 that superseded the HP O/100 had many improved features but principally, more power virtue Rolls-Royce Eagle VIIIs.

A large airplane, it could carry a crew of three—the pilot, an observer, and a gunlayer as well as one of the largest aerial bombs of World War One, the 1650 pounder. Garrie's mission reports note that his usual ordnance load consisted of sixteen 112 lb high explosive (HE) and ten 25 lb Cooper bombs.

As Garrie's story unfolded under the scrutiny of our research, it proved hard not to be emotionally angered by the scale and nature of the WW I losses of young folk trapped in a type of warfare that bears little of the science, intent or account found in modern conflict (terrible as it too certainly is, in its own way) but was simply attritional and properly, if darkly, described by the metaphor of "meat grinder." Rudyard Kipling's great 1897 poem, the "Recessional" returns to the refrain in four stanzas, "Lest we forget—lest we forget" and is an admonishment to be careful not to forget those things of great value to any nation. After the great sacrifices of WW I, these words passed into common usage for Remembrance Day observations and, as often as not, as the only epitaph on war memorials that were found in most every urban community in Britain, Northern Ireland and the Commonwealth. Well, our research into Garrie's air war banished the abstraction of this conflict and it has been the strongest reminder that our family's loss remains a deep wound, that we should not and do not forget. The Arras Flying Services Memorial to the Missing holds a memorial to almost one thousand airmen with no known grave, and the memorial is in the grounds of the Arras Memorial commemorating nearly thirty-five thousand names of the fallen. The Flying Services Memorial is adjacent to the Stone of Remembrance with the poignant reminder "Their Names Liveth for Evermore" carved on both of the two long sides. An irony is that Garrie probably flew close to what would become the site of this memorial as he completed missions in nearby Cambrai, Douai and along the Cambrai-Arras road. He is also memorialized on plaques in the Hitchin Grammar School Library, UK, East Anglian School entrance hall, Bury St. Edmunds, UK, and the Hitchin War Memorial adjacent to St. Mary's Church in Hitchin, Hertfordshire, UK

So from the R.N.V.R., Garrie completed basic training flying the Farman (maybe the MF7), the Avro 504 and the Royal Aircraft Factory BE-2c machines, with the rank of Temporary Probationary Flying Officer. Thanks to Toni and Ray Fow, I have flown in two open-cockpit biplanes—the Waco F Series and the de Havilland Tiger Moth. Part way through Garrie's training on 1 April, 1918, the Royal Air Force, R.A.F. was established from the amalgamation of the R.N.A.S. and the Royal Flying Corps, R.F.C. So, he became one of the founder members of the R.A.F., one among 300,000 service men and some women and 20,000 planes. Garrie's rank became Probationary Second Lieutenant, R.A.F. He graduated as a Temporary Second Lieutenant in May, 1918—assessed to have Flying ability 1st class with 55 hours and 28 minutes flying time and results of 2nd class/Wireless Telegraphy 96.6%: 1st class/Photography 96.6%. After basic and operational flying training, Garrie joined 215 Squadron as they were being re-equipped and retrained with HP O/400s at Andover in Hampshire. On many occasions, when young and sitting in the back of Mum and Dad's car, I travelled past the Andover airfield. From there he traveled to Alquines in north-eastern France. He must have done many training missions, but in the absence of his flying log book, none of these acclimating flights are recorded. However, each of his night bombing missions is recorded on the Squadron after-action Mission Reports. Also available for research are the Operation Orders published on the day of the Mission. His main targets were enemy aerodromes including Buhl, Boulay and Frescaty and railway junctions at Metz-Sablon, Ehrang and Courcelles.

Other than the military documentation held in the National Archives, Kew, UK, as noted above, the only family heirloom relating to Garrie is his memorial plaque. This was issued to next-of-kin with a scroll. Sadly we have no photographs—only a picture of fresh-faced youths at Hitchin Boys Grammar School in 1908. It is more than likely that Garrie is one of the nine-year-old students there.

We can never know Garrie's actual response to flying into adversity—many times in adverse weather conditions and under fire. Particular commentary on his very low-level bombing at night demonstrates that he was a skilled and daring airman, and the medical grounding of his usual observer shows that this could not have been without drawing on nervous fortitude. On the night of September 16/17, 1918, Garrie returned to Xaffévillers Aerodrome with his airplane D4568 damaged so badly that it would take many hours to repair, as shown in the records. There are no reports of his final flight in Handley page C9732 except the German soldier who retrieved his personal possessions and returned them to England. It was recounted second-hand from an eye-witness that the airplane crash landed and there followed an explosion, but neither its location nor the exact cause of the crash was given. The witness, a German soldier wrote, "I was at my post when I saw him landing. At the same moment I heard a fearful explosion, and when I was able to get near, I found him dead under his aeroplane." His sister was notified of his death and the information that he was buried in the Garrison Cemetery in Metz, then in Germany, now in France. However, the Commonwealth War Graves Commission has no record of Garrie's grave, or that of his crew. Many before him and many since, have followed orders that led to their deaths.

With no actual pictures of Garrie available—so far—we have commissioned a painting of Garrie's HP O/400 over the aerodrome at Frescaty with the historically correct Zeppelin hangar and Casino de Frescaty. Artist Neil Hipkiss, GAvA, has captured the drama of his final very low-altitude west-east attack on the Frescaty enemy aerodrome with hangar and Casino depicted as they were in 1918.

I have been a volunteer at the Smithsonian Institution National Air and Space Museum in Washington D.C. and Chantilly, Virginia, USA since 2003. I have a variety of interests in aerospace—particularly the science relating to aircraft and spacecraft. There are two artifacts on display at the National Air and Space Museum's Steven F. Udvar-Hazy Center in Chantilly, Virginia of particular interest because of their connection to Uncle Garrie. I always view the French twin-engined light bomber with a little poignancy since it is the most similar World War One airplane to the H.P. O/400 in the Museum. The Caudron G4 had a wingspan barely half that of Garrie's H.P. O/400. Sadly, there are no remaining Handley Page O/400s in existence. Only propellers and a wing fragment in storage at the R.A.F. Museum, Cosford, Shropshire, UK and a small piece of propeller looking more like a few inches of 2 x 4 displayed at the Shuttleworth Collection in Old Warden, Bedfordshire, UK. On the opposite side of the aisle to the Caudron G4 in the National Air and Space Museum's Steven F. Udvar-Hazy Center in Chantilly, Virginia, USA, is a Halberstadt CL.IV. It was a ground-strike aircraft in 1918 but used on moonlit nights near the end of WWI, like the full moon of September 20, 1918, against night bombers of the Independent Force. Garrie's 215 Squadron was one of nine squadrons in Major-General Hugh Trenchard's Independent Force. The Museum's Halberstadt CL.IV was donated by a WWI German pilot, Paul Strähle, who served with Jagdstaffel 18. His squadron was flying out of Montigen less than 10 miles east of Metz. Frescaty Aerodrome, the location of Garrie's last mission is a few miles south-west of Metz.

The squadron badge depicts a porcupine with the motto "Surgite nox adest," which translates into "Arise, night is at hand." On the moonlit night of 20th September, 1918, as on many evenings when he set out on bombing missions, Garrie did, indeed, arise as night approached. He took off at 8.08 p.m. with Frescaty Aerodrome as the target. For Garrie and his crew, it was the last time they would respond to the squadron's call.

In this book we have tried to present Garrie's story as best it is known. We have included facts and sources as we have found them and hope that this provides the reader with useful historical context. Where there has been an absence of facts, we have joined the points with only so much licence as may be reasonable by the standards of likely WW I military aviation. And, whether Garrie and his observer did suck 'humbug' sweets/candies when settled into the mission….who knows?

C.G.H. April, 2018

Handley Page O/400 Night Bomber Pilot

Between 19:43 and 21:00 on the evening of 20 September, 1918, four Handley Page O/400s launched from their Xaffévillers Aerodrome base as the night's first bombing wave and their mission was to attack the Frescaty aerodrome, a German fighter facility and sometime operating airfield for the Richthofen Jagdstaffel 11. The staged take-off of the four 215 Squadron aircraft was planned to de-conflict their individual arrival times over the Frescaty aerodrome target and, thereby, to stretch enemy air defences; additionally, separation was standard operational practice for the night bombing squadrons to lessen the danger of take-off or in flight collisions.

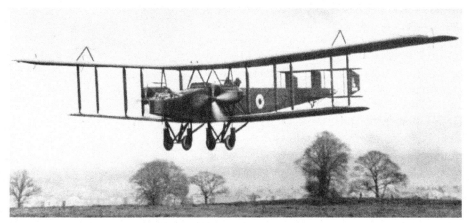

Figure 1; Handley Page O/400 landing at RAF Andover, Wiltshire, United Kingdom 1918
(Public Domain - Prior Jan 1, 1923)

The third O/400 to taxi was C9732 and it left the ground at 20:08 manned by three-aircrew and carrying fourteen 112 lb high explosive bombs. Following a period of poor, wet weather, the night was clear with visibility reported to be excellent over the target; below ~7,000 feet, 1/10 altostratus cloud cover. Handley Page squadrons of the Independent Force preferred to operate during the week-long periods of full moons, and in September 1918, the moon waxed on 16/17 September, with 50 percent full-moon brightness and above through to 23/24 September. On 20 September, there was a full moon shining and good visibility but a strong wind was freshening from the west.

No. 215 Squadron Royal Air Force (R.A.F.) was formed in France on 1 April, 1918, by renumbering No. 15 squadron of the Royal Naval Air Service

(R.N.A.S.) which, less than a month earlier on 10 March, 1918, had been established at Coudekerque, near Dunkirk. The squadron operated the Handley Page O/100 in the role of night bomber to attack strategic targets in Germany. Night operations were more technically demanding of airmanship and dangerous to fly than in daylight, as was captured in the prevailing wisdom of the day which observed with no little irony, "Flying at night is no different from flying in the daytime, except you can't see."[1] Almost immediately after forming as 215, the squadron returned to England to re-equip with the improved Handley Page O/400 (figure 1) before, again, deploying to France on 4 July. It was based in Alquines and was designated as part of the Independent Air Force. The Independent Force was established under the leadership of Major-General Hugh Trenchard and comprised four day (55(DH-4), 99 and 104(DH-9) and 110(DH-9A)) and four Handley Page O/400 night squadrons (97, 115, 215 and 216). Additionally 100 Squadron was included as a fifth night squadron flying F.E.2Bs and would re-equip with Handley Page O/400 in August.

Figure 2: No. 215 Squadron Crest
R.A.F. Public Domain)

The Independent Force goal was established to prove the value of strategic, heavy bombing – namely the destruction of war making capability such as materials manufacturing capability; blast furnaces, coal and iron mining and chemical production. However, Trenchard, expanded the Independent Force mission to include such tactical targets as rail junctions and enemy airfields. The intensity of operations increased with the beginning of the Allied ground offensive on 8 August with the Battle of Amiens. 215 Squadron, under the command of Major John Fleming Jones[2], began offensive night operations in July 1918 from Alquines but moved to a new base of operations, Xaffévillers, (figure 3), on 19 August. Xaffévillers aerodrome was sited

---

[1] From Biplanes and Bombsights British Bombing in World War I by George K. Williams (1999) quoting Ralph R. Williams, "Navigation: From Dead Reckoning to Navstar GPS,"AirForce Magazine 67, no. 12 (December 1984)

[2] Jones was one of the earliest Handley Page pilots and had crewed the first O/100 that flew in France in November 1916. Although squadron Commanding Officers were not approved to fly operationally, Jones did fly and by November 1918, he had flown on forty operations over enemy lines.

Figure 3: The site of Xaffévillers aerodrome today ~100 years later
(courtesy Google Maps © 2018)

9

Figure 4: War Damage at the Church in Xaffévillers in 1914-15 from a
postcard (copyright expired)

approximately twelve miles east of the front lines and was shared with 100 Squadron who by later September had converted to HP-O/400s.

The Handley Page O/400 C9732 was crewed by pilot 2nd Lieutenant Alfred Charles Garrett ("ACG" in the squadron and "Garrie" to his family) Fowler, observer 2nd Lieutenant Clement Clough Eaves and gunlayer 2nd Lieutenant John Shannon Ferguson. This crew had not previously flown together operationally; however, any unfamiliarity involved, was not unusual. Although crews endeavored to build some operational continuity by staying together over a number of missions, attrition and the need to familiarize new arrivals to the battlespace resulted in necessary changes to crew composition. For example, newly arrived pilots or observers would often fly qualifying missions as a gunlayer to build familiarity with operating theater and procedures. Both Eaves and Ferguson were newly qualified observers and had joined Independent Force, 215 Squadron, together, barely two weeks earlier on 8 September, 1918.

Figure 5: Handley Page O/400 No. 1 Squadron, Australian Flying Corps at Haifa, North Palestine, Ottoman Empire, in 1918 the (Public Domain – 25-year term of copyright has expired - Australian Copyright Council)

Comparatively, the Handley Page O series (figure 5) was a metaphoric flying 'Kraken'[3] in the skies of WW I - it was the largest aircraft that had been built

---

[3] The massive creature exulted by Alfred Tennyson's irregular 1830 sonnet

by Britain[4]. Conceived by the aircraft company Handley Page under a proposal submitted in December 1914, a prototype aircraft first flew at Hendon on 17 December, 1915. It was configured as a biplane with 100-foot wingspan and overhanging upper-wing surfaces, braced struts, and a biplane empennage with balanced rudders between the horizontal surfaces. The rectangular fuselage was 62.7 feet long and it accommodated three separate aircrew positions and an internal bomb-bay. It was fitted with two engines driving four-bladed propellers between the horizontal wing surfaces. Built in two principal variants, the Handley Page O/100 and the later more powerful Handley Page O/400, the power-plants were respectively two 260 horsepower Rolls-Royce Eagle II engines and two 360 horsepower Eagle VIII engines. Its maximum speed was 97.5 mph, cruise speed ~65 mph and stall speed, ~53 mph - maximum range was ~700 miles, service ceiling 8,500 feet and rate of climb, 23 minutes to 5,000 ft. The O/400 empty weight was 8,502 lb with maximum take-off weight 13,360 lb and this enabled a bomb load up to 2,000 lb and five 0.303 in (7.7 mm) Lewis Guns; nose (2), dorsal (2) and ventral hatch (1) positions. Able to carry a maximum of sixteen 112 lb bombs mounted vertically in a sort of upside down milk bottle crate, the observer had one lever to remotely remove safety pins to allow air priming of the bombs and a second lever to turn a drum attached to wires that released the bombs either singly or in groups. If a bomb failed to release, the gunlayer in the rear cockpit would be expected to kick it free. The Handley Page was a heavy aircraft to fly and was described notably by Cecil Lewis, the WW 1 fighter pilot and author of *Sagittarius Rising,* as "it was like a lorry in the air. When you decided to turn left, you pushed over the controls, went and had a cup of tea and came back to find the turn just starting." Nevertheless, O/400 crews had confidence in their aircraft believing them to be capable of absorbing punishment under fire and structurally 'sturdy'. Heavy landings at night on return from raids were relatively common due to landing difficulty caused by a policy requiring severest airfield illumination 'blackout' - so a sturdy aircraft design was considered a blessing. It was in July 1918 at Netheravon, when 215 Squadron re-equipped with the HP O/400 aircraft that, newly qualified pilot 2nd Lieutenant Fowler, who had just turned nineteen years of age on the 17 June joined squadron strength.

---

[4] The Handley Page 'O' series design was initiated under an Admiralty requirement issued in December 1914 with the Director of the Air Department (Royal Navy), Captain Murray Sueter, stating his need to Frederick Handley Page for a long range bomber and possibly coining the descriptive phrase that it should be "a bloody paralyser of an aircraft." The prototype aircraft flew one year later on 7 December, 1915.

As pilot of Handley Page C9732 on 20 September, Garrie Fowler was embarking on his thirteenth bombing mission as aircraft captain since qualifying operational in early August - he had also flown as gunlayer on an additional five missions to familiarize with the terrain at night in the area of squadron operations and to accustom himself with the effects of searchlights and various enemy anti-aircraft fires. As a general rule, newly joined pilots might be required to fly up to seven missions as a gunlayer to accrue qualifying experience. Fowler flew four of these missions as gunlayer for the veteran 215 Squadron pilot, Captain G.S. Buck MC, DFC, who, sadly, was killed landing his Handley Page on the night of 2 September, crashing into a fuel store on the airfield after an operation – Buck was 21-years old at the time and had previously served with the British Expeditionary Force in 1914 for 16-months before transferring to the R.F.C. and flying scout fighter aircraft where he won his MC; he transferred to fly Handley Pages in April 1918. By 20 September, Fowler was considered to be an experienced and capable pilot and had earned peer respect within the squadron for his daring low-level bombing in pursuit of night targeting accuracy. All told, he had flown twenty-one missions including raids on four aerodromes, namely, Folsperwiller, Boulay, Buhl and Morhange. He had not, however, raided Frescaty aerodrome previously.

By early 1917, the Royal Naval Air Service and the Royal Flying Corps efforts to conduct strategic bombing campaigns had led the Government to conclude that there was value in the creation of an independent Royal Air Force incorporating a separate independent strategic strike force. This last became known as the 'Independent Force' and comprised day and night bomber units, whose sole purpose was to attack strategic[5] targets in Germany and, thereby, to damage the German materiel war effort. The campaigns to be conducted by the Independent Force involved no requirement to report to or to coordinate efforts with either the Army or Navy. The Royal Air Force was established on 1 April, 1918, and the Independent Force under the command of Major General Hugh Trenchard[6] on 6 June of the same year.

---

[5] Strategic targets were agreed between the British and French Governments and transmitted through the Supreme War Council to the American and Italian Governments under the Heads of Agreement as to the Constitution of the Inter-Allied Independent Air Force, 3 October, 1918, and were summed up as with the objective, "To carry war into Germany by attacking her industry, commerce and population."

[6] Trenchard was appointed Chief of the Air Staff on 18 January, 1918 after being recruited to the post by the newspaper proprietor Lord Rothermere, who was himself a recent appointment as Air Minister to the newly established department in November 1917. He clashed quickly with Rothermere over issues including the Air Minister's inexperience, matters of military management and future air-power policy. Matters came to a head and Trenchard resigned on 19 March triggered by a spat between the two men

Trenchard's appointment solved the problem of what to do with him after his contentious April 1918 resignation but it also appears to have involved a number of interpersonal tensions not only with the existing service Chiefs but also within the Royal Air Force (R.A.F.) command. His Independent Force command was freed of interference by the R.A.F. Chief of the Air Staff, Frederick Sykes, by the simple bypass measure that required him to report solely and directly to the British Air Minister, Sir William Weir. Weir did not appear to exercise any effective oversight or scrutiny over Independent Force operations and, apparently, neither did Trenchard feel burdened by a personal obligation to be thoroughly candid with him. He reported strategic operations to the Air Minister but in his operational orders to squadrons, he included prioritized tactical targets such as railways and aerodromes. Essentially, he was free to develop the Independent Force mission subject only to his own predispositions. Trenchard drove his Independent Force squadron commanders relentlessly in a ruthless attritional method of air-war fighting. With night bombing expertise still in its infancy, it was abundantly clear that achieving target destruction or worthwhile material damage was very difficult. This was because of the short-comings of 1918 aircraft technology which included for example, marginal aircraft flying qualities, adverse weather limitations, night-navigation difficulty, target accuracy challenges and very limited airborne situational awareness at night. Overall, it might be said that the weather was the final arbiter of whether launching an operation was practicable. There was a clear need to balance the heavy losses of Independent Force aircraft and trained aircrew, which accumulated during the summer of 1918 at a startling rate, against the value of destruction caused to enemy facilities and material. In short, balanced against losses, were the results worthwhile? If his aircrews were sensitive to this balance in warfare, Trenchard himself took a less nuanced view and he admonished the 216 Squadron Commander to "get them (216 aircrew) out of the ideas," which included not flying in unsuitable weather. Launching in conditions that denied any reasonable possibility of reaching a target, let alone bombing accurately, seems to have been what Trenchard

over allocation of air assets to the Western Front. However, at Rothermere's request, he agreed to defer the date of his departure until after 1 April when the Royal Air Force would officially stand up. In the convulsive row that followed, King George and the Cabinet became involved with the result that sympathy for Trenchard tilted in his favour leading to Rothermere himself to resign on 25 April. New Air Minister, Sir William Weir, was immediately under pressure to accommodate Trenchard in a new position. Trenchard played coy believing that the jobs that Weir offered to him were artificial having neither responsibility nor authority commensurate with his standing. Eventually, Trenchard relented and was appointed General Officer Commanding the Independent Air Force on 15 June, 1918 and was headquartered in Nancy, France.

demanded in order to generate dubiously favorable raiding statistics based on large numbers of missions conducted rather than enemy materiel destruction. Independent Force losses due to enemy action were severely high for the day squadrons. While no one should question Trenchard's own history of personal courage and fortitude, his seemingly unscientific resolution to bomb at any cost appears to have led to a level of wastage of aircrew and machines that simply appeared materially profligate; made bitter by the pain associated with individual loss of life. Furthermore, the scale of losses eventually led to a need to suspend some operations because squadrons simply ran out of aircraft and aircrew. A more judicious exercise of these resources would likely have achieved much the same destructive effect on enemy facilities but with lower attrition of Independent Force capability. The reporting "bubble" that Trenchard established around himself (i.e. accountable to the Air Minister alone), relieved him of detailed scrutiny by ranking peers. Some will argue that the Independent Force losses were worthwhile no matter whether wasteful of air materiel because they were collateral to sustaining the case to establish the value of strategic bombing and this led directly to the strike forces of today. However, "attritional" warfare as a philosophy has long been discredited because, left unchecked, losses eventually undermine all ability to continue military engagement with opposing forces. All else aside, the crews of the Independent Force, likely skeptical of the wit and aero-operational understanding of their "rear-echelon" generals, committed to battle irrespectively, as young men of action most often do. When the weather resulted in low visibility over the target, they might descend to extremely low altitude; bombing at night from a height of 75 feet. Flying two missions in one evening, subjected to enemy fire a second time, undoubtedly drew heavily on their visceral fortitude. And in some cases, being forced to return prematurely with engine trouble, they opted to land in a risky heavy state in order to conserve their ordnance for a later try despite being in near pitch black darkness. The sustained commitment by the Independent Force aircrews from June to November 1918, in the face of horrific losses (e.g. 55 Squadron (day) July-September losses: 125%; 215 Squadron (night) June-November: 120%), was quite remarkable. If Trenchard brooked no 'namby-pamby' reluctance by his squadron commanders to launch attacks even under the most unfavorable circumstances, despite morale sapping losses, his aircrew remained up for the fight so long as there were sufficient in numbers to fly. Drawing on Tennyson's great poem written sixty four years earlier, the aircrew of the Independent Force could rightly claim "honour the charge they made!"

15

Five days earlier on evening of 15 September, piloting his own Handley Page D4568, Garrie Fowler flew two sorties from Xaffévillers to raid the enemy aerodrome at Buhl. His observer was 2ⁿᵈ Lieutenant Thomas Victor Preedy, who was twenty-three years of age and had flown with him several times during September, and they had likely developed some operational rapport. Acting as gunlayer that evening was 2ⁿᵈ Lieutenant Hugh Reginald Dodd (Figure 6), a pilot newly arrived at 215 and flying this evening to acquire ground and operational theater familiarization. First take-off was at 19:34 and, arriving over Buhl aerodrome around 25 minutes later, they made a W to E run across the aerodrome and released their bombs. They followed this making a strafing run at 200 feet, targeting the hangar and aircraft on the ground. They reported facing 'flaming green onions' (FGO) on the approach and intense machine-gun (MG) fire and searchlights. Recovering safely to Xaffévillers at 21:10, D4568 was refueled and re-armed and took off again to raid Buhl a second time at 21:53. Approaching from the W, although there was some ground mist building up, visibility at 100 feet height was good. Fowler descended to a height of 70 feet and made a successful very low bombing run. Circling and running W to E, the aircraft made a follow-on strafing run at 100 feet high and took intense ground fires from anti-aircraft (AA), MG and FGO. D4568 was badly damaged. The after action report noted that it was

Figure 6: Lt Hugh Reginald Dodd RN, 215 Squadron, killed in action 16 September 1918 (copyright expired)

"riddled" by tracer and "ball ammunition" with the main fuel line shot away, one elevator badly smashed...lateral (aileron) controls hit and port bottom main-plane very badly riddled. Control of the aircraft on the return flight was accomplished only with great difficulty and the pilot evidently demonstrated exceptional airmanship to recover to Xaffévillers and land safely. The aircraft was reported to be so badly damaged that it was

16

withdrawn for deep repair. Somewhat surprisingly, in view of the fire taken by D4568, the three-aircrew were not reported wounded and all were to fly again within a few days. It is hard not to conclude that after the euphoria of a safe return against some very short-odds had subsided, they were not a little shaken by the events of these two raids. Dodd was to fly again on the following evening, 16 September, piloting his own Handley Page C9658, which was to be one of four aircraft of five launched that that failed to return in a disastrous night for 215 Squadron. Regrettably, although Dodd's crew survived the attack, were captured and made prisoners of war, he himself was killed in the crash landing; he was aged nineteen. Returning to 2nd Lieutenant Fowler - likely in consideration of his efforts on the evening 15 September, his next-of-kin were later informed that he was recommended for a decoration, however, his death in action a few days later necessarily, but sadly, resulted in the award process being discontinued.

Following the Franco-Prussian war of 1870, France ceded parts of Lorraine to Germany under the Treaty of Frankfurt which was signed on 10 May, 1871. The garrison city of Metz and nearby Frescaty in Lorraine became part of the Imperial German territory of Alsace-Lorraine. Lying close to the new frontier and strategically significant, Metz was of commercial importance, possessed a rail complex as well

Figure 7: Frescaty aerodrome around April 1919 - In the center, the Zeppelin hangar followed by the Casino de Frescaty, second hangar and two sets of aircraft sheds. (Photograph by Maurice Lepleux, 1919)

as the nearby navigable River Moselle/canal. With suitable local geography, a Zeppelin airship base was established in 1909 in the grounds adjacent to the Casino de Frescaty; a grand house built between 1710 and 1714 (later to be destroyed during Second World War by American bombing). A large hangar capable of housing a 150-meter LZ3 Zeppelin was constructed at the

Figure 8: The Casino de Frescaty (1918) at the aerodrome from a postcard (copyright expired) (upper) and Zeppelin Hangar at Frescaty Aerodrome (Public Domain - Image from the National Library of France) (lower)

18

site and a year later, in 1910, it became an airfield and training base for future pilots of the Imperial German Army Air Service (Luftstreitkräfte). From August 1914, Frescaty aerodrome conducted Zeppelin operations and observation balloon training. By mid-1916, Frescaty aerodrome was operating AEG.GI-IV bombers, Rumpler CI-III two-seater reconnaissance biplanes and Halberstadt D-type fighters. Subsequently, with the emergence of new Albatros and Fokker fighter-scout aircraft, a number of Jagdstaffel (fighter/hunter staffel (squadron)) operated from Frescaty aerodrome until war's end. Recognizing its military importance, as part of the Metz sector, Frescaty became the target of repeated French air attacks. Additionally, the nearby Metz-Sablon rail junction triangle grew in importance during the ongoing hostilities because the whole of the Verdun front was resupplied by the railways passing through it. By later 1918, 215 Squadron considered Metz anti-aircraft defences to be the 'hottest' spot along the front with perhaps as many as 80 anti-aircraft guns and 30 searchlights. From the air, the Frescaty aerodrome was dominated by the Zeppelin hangar to the north. In a contiguous line to the south east from this hangar lay the Casino de Frescaty, a second significant hangar and two files of fighter-scout aircraft sheds (figure 7). To the south of the airfield were additional aircraft facilities and anti-aircraft (AA) dispositions. Trenchard, as noted earlier made a number of aerodromes priority targets for his squadrons and by the end of hostilities, Frescaty alone was bombed six times in daylight raids and fourteen times by night by the Independent Force. Overall, 215 Squadron played a significant part in mounting aerodrome night bombing and strafing attacks including several on Frescaty from late August until the end of hostilities in November 1918.

As noted earlier, Fowler's crew members on the evening of 20 September were Eaves and Ferguson. His aircraft, C9732, was a new machine that had been taken on charge by the squadron only a few days earlier, on 17 September. On the night of 20 September, following operations on 15 September, Preedy, Fowler's usual observer, was allocated fly with another pilot, 2/Lieutenant Buckle in Handley Page D9680. However, D9680 encountered engine trouble and aborted the night's operation. Preedy was only to fly one more time and this was on 21 September in Handley Page C9714. Sadly, after the series of squadron losses, his nerves were probably shot through and he was hospitalized and declared indefinitely unfit for flying; a victim of operational flying fatigue. Clement Clough Eaves was 24-years old and hailed from Stockport, Cheshire. Trained as an aero-engineer and working at the Mirrlees engine company, he joined the Royal Flying

Corps on 3 April, 1917 but was placed on a reserve list known as Class W (Army) Reserve, since his services were deemed to be more valuable to the country in his engineering employment rather than serving in uniform. With mounting war losses, he was called on to "Rejoin the Colors" on 25 March, 1918, transferred to Royal Air Force service on 1 April and underwent aircrew selection being assessed unsuitable for pilot training on 9 April. However, found fit for observer, Eaves underwent observer training at Blackdown, Surrey, through August 1918, with night training completed by 10 August and award of 'operationally qualified observer' on 23 August. He

joined 215 Squadron in France on the 8 September and it is quite likely that he had a week's leave before this. Although he will have had familiarization and check-out flights after joining 215, when he took off at 20:08 on 20 September as observer for C9732, it was his first operational mission. John Shannon Ferguson (figure 9) was also an observer and joined the Independent Force, 215 Squadron on the same day as Eaves. Ferguson was Scots-American and his parents lived in Pittsfield, Massachusetts, USA. Twenty-four years old, he had most recently lived in Hawick, Scotland and was employed in the rubber industry. He was gazetted, confirmed as 2/Lieutenant on 7 September, 1918. Although flying as gunlayer and not observer, his circumstances on the evening of 20 September mirrored those of Eaves. The gunlayer crew position was isolated in the Handley Page O/400 with no

Figure 9: 2nd Lieutenant John Shannon Ferguson RAF, 215 Squadron killed in action 20 September 1918
(copyright expired)

voice communication with the pilot and observer. A wire line between front and rear cockpits could pull messages from back to front but fur lined gauntlets made its handling somewhat impracticable.

The Handley Page O/400 had no on-board navigation equipment other than a compass and clock to assist aircrew in finding their way to a target in darkness during the night hours. Other than the occasional glimpse of a river or rail line that might be weakly illuminated by moonshine and 'dead reckoning' dependent on map-reading skills, there was not much else. In the cockpit, the pilot flew the aircraft from the right-hand seat and the observer would sit in the left seat except when bomb aiming or to man the front cockpit Lewis gun for air defence or ground strafing. Accessing the front cockpit required a tortuous crawl forward (figure 10). The pilot's cockpit

Figure 10: The observer and pilot in a Handley Page O/400: Observer in the nose cockpit, manning a single Lewis gun mounted on a Scarff ring near Cressy, 25 September 1918: Photograph by 2nd Lieutenant David McLellan (Public Domain - United Kingdom Government and taken prior to 1 June 1957)

instrumentation included an altimeter, compass, air speed indicator, clock, radiator thermometers and a curved spirit-level bank indicator – to the right on the fuselage was the differential engine throttle and just above the throttle lever, an altitude-control adjuster for the engine carburation. The Elliott engine revolutions counter and temperature indicator were mounted on the inside of the engine nacelles and the observer assisted in monitoring them along with adjustment of the radiator shutter opening in order to maintain temperatures of between 60 to 70^0 C. If the Handley Page offered some flying challenges because of limited flight aids, night flying presented an additional gauntlet to run as diminished situational awareness and disorientating 'leans' might compromise airborne safety. The Handley Page O/400s were not equipped to fly in poor weather and they were particularly vulnerable to deteriorating meteorological conditions (e.g. a freshening return head wind) during an operation. This could increase the risk of not making a safe return to base.... if not make it completely impossible. Independent Force Handley Page night flying aircrew were twice as likely as day operators to be casualties of flying accidents although they were four to five times less likely to be casualties of hostile fire engagements.

The return flight from bombing raids was to some extent assisted by the provision of Allied navigation aids which were known colloquially as the 'lighthouses'. Lighthouses were high-powered electric light-emitting beacons located at between 15 to 25 kilometers behind the front lines and spaced 30 kilometers apart. They flashed a recognizable sequence of Morse code letters that could provide a navigational fix for aircrews at night. The light emitted by these beacons might be visible for up to as much as 100 kilometers under favorable visual atmospheric conditions.

From 1915, the need for more acute target accuracy when bombing was well recognized by the R.F.C Command. It was determined that, with the limited size of the bombs that could be carried by aircraft of the time, ordnance needed to be placed within a radius of 50 feet of the target to cause sufficient critical damage. If on-target accuracy could not be achieved from the somewhat safer operating heights of around 6000 feet (less vulnerable to anti-aircraft fire), targets needed to be attacked at low levels down to 500 feet. Although high-level bombing provided less exposure to enemy anti-aircraft defences and was therefore eminently desirable, it was not enabled by the existing bomb-sight technology, which even by later 1918 was still basic and not easy to use in the air and was consequently not effective. The result was that bombing effectiveness was generally poor. Indeed, in the inclement weather conditions encountered and at safer high altitudes, aircrews experienced difficulties in hitting targets smaller than a large town! The Mk I High Altitude Drift Sight used on the O/400 was mounted on the fuselage nose and was awkward for the bomb aimer observer to use.

Although the Drift Sight was a significant improvement over earlier designs, it still required the aircraft to fly directly into wind with the observer inputting altitude and forward speed. Aircrews found that low-level bombing by 'eyeball' achieved better bombing accuracy. With that old maxim, "no good deed ever goes unpunished" and, perhaps unsurprisingly, Handley Page Independent Force aircrews came under intense pressure from Command to bomb at low level in order to improve bombing results irrespective of increased risk to men and machines.

As has been noted, Trenchard pursued a very aggressive offensive policy for the Independent Force despite extremely high losses of aircraft and aircrew. Maj W. R. Read, who was preparing to take over 216 Squadron recorded that Trenchard had said to him, "I have got you out here to take over 216 Squadron. They have got 'Naval' ideas. They think they cannot fly at night if there is a cloud in the sky and they think they cannot do more than one raid in a night. You have got to get them out of those ideas." The type of heavily attritional offensive campaign that Trenchard conducted could only be supported by a massive input of replacement aircrew and aircraft. By 1917, the quality of British aircraft had improved (noting that between March and May 1917, the R.F.C. lost 1270 aeroplanes and what turned the tide for the R.F.C. during the remainder of the war was the introduction of more capable new aircraft such as the S.E.5a scout, the Bristol F.2B "Brisfit" fighter and the DH-4 – the latter being the series flown by the Independent Force day-bomber squadrons). However, pilot and observer training were still inadequate for the demands made upon them. There seems to be little doubt that Trenchard was content to accept a high attrition so long as he could continue to launch Independent Force bombing raids to damage enemy morale and against his preferred tactical targets. Although evidently a leader able to drive his squadrons into action (until squadron aircrew and aircraft numbers fell so precipitously that squadrons were robbed of warfighting cohesion), there seems to have been little scientific or technical assessment or the need to balance benefit with loss in his war-fighting reasoning. It is hard not to escape the conclusion that Trenchard was demanding that his Independent Force aircrews bridge the gap in operational and equipment shortcomings with their personal courage and sense of duty.

In early September 1918, Trenchard further diverted his Independent Force raiding priority from the mandate of strategic missions to the tactical support of the United States led attack on the long-entrenched German St. Mihiel Salient. Between 12 and 15 September he launched multiple bombing raids on aerodromes and the Metz-Sablon railway triangle. The weather on the eleventh was poor with driving rain and wind and no flying by 215 aircraft was possible. By Thursday the twelfth, it was still raining for much of the day and, although the wind was down to 10 to 15 mph at the ground and gusting, at operating altitude it was reaching 50 mph. Nevertheless, Trenchard was becoming increasingly anxious that night attacks be launched to make an allied contribution to the American effort. Between 13 and 15 September, 215 Squadron launched a number of attacks despite visibility remaining exceedingly poor, the result of thick cloud banks and moon-dim, dense darkness. Very low flight[7] was required to distinguish targets. 2nd Lieutenant Fowler flew missions on each of these evenings and, as noted above, on 15 September, his Handley Page aircraft D4568 was very heavily damaged by enemy fire while conducting very low-level bombing runs. After this evening, he was apparently rested for four nights and was not operational again until 20 September and, thereby, he missed being part of the disastrous loss of four 215 Squadron aircraft on 16 September.

At 16:30 on 20 September, 83rd Wing Royal Air Force operational Order No. 73 (see page 62) had been issued to the five Handley Page Independent Force night bomber squadrons to allocate their targets for that night. The order was classified 'Secret' and as a controlled document, 215 Squadron received copy number four. The order was simple and required "All available Handley Pages to attack the Hostile Aerodrome at Frescaty. Time of start: 7:15 p.m." Also it is noteworthy that under the same order, sister 216 Squadron was required to send two Handley Pages to attack the Lanz Works at Mannheim and all other remaining squadron aircraft to join in the raid on Frescaty with the same 7:15 pm launch time. There is no mention of a requirement to conduct a second wave of operations with a hot refuel and re-arm on return after a first mission but it is likely that this was understood to be the case if assessed operationally favorable at the time. All available aircraft for 215 Squadron proved to be just four Handley Pages, namely D9680 (19:43), C9724 (19:50), C9732 (20:08) and C9434 (21:00) and their

---

[7] 215 Squadron Commander Major J.F. Jones, on the 7 October 1918, was recommended for mention in Despatches with the commendation that, "This officer has done exceedingly good work whilst Commanding No. 215 Squadron. It is very largely owing to Major Jones that the Pilots of this Squadron consistently come down low to bomb their objective, and frequently make 2 and 3 trips in one night." Along with policy for squadron commanders, Jones did not fly combat missions during the period June-October 1918 but, evidently, he provided the leadership drive for his pilots to fly low and to fly multiple missions in one night. Given the 120% loss rate of 215 Squadron, Jones's mindset can only be imagined. Certainly, 2nd Lieutenant Fowler responded to the Squadron low-flying directive and he developed a reputation for daring; ultimately, this most likely contributed to his and his crew's fate over Frescaty.

pilots were, respectively, Buckle, Darnton, Fowler and Kestell. After take-off, D9680 encountered engine problems and returned to Xaffévillers, landing at 20:23. After rectification work was carried out on the Handley Page engine on the ground, it relaunched at 21:25 only to suffer a recurrence of the problem and landed at 21:35 aborting any further attempts that night. Darnton (C9724) and Kestell (C9434) returned safely from the first operation at 21:40 and 21:50 respectively having mission flight times of around 1:50 hours. Both aircraft were refueled and re-armed and relaunched at 23:20 and 23:47; they conducted successful second raids on Frescaty recovering to Xaffévillers at 00:55 and 02:15 on the morning of 21 September.

After every raid on enemy territory, 215 Squadron returning aircrews were debriefed by the squadron intelligence officer (SIO). A debriefing form was prepared prior to take-off with header details that comprised pilot and aircrew details, aircraft number and date but otherwise, it was left blank. The form was usually filled out in advance by a squadron NCO and presented to the SIO for him to make a written record during the aircrew mission debrief. The SIO for 215 usually wrote in pencil and recorded details of the raid – times, weather, bombs dropped, results and the resistance met, et cetera. Catching aircrew fresh, immediately on return from their mission, was essential so as to avoid forgetting important details. However, sensitivity was probably required with the potential for a full range of emotions on display ranging from elation to fright. When an aircraft did not return, the SIO would write on the form nothing more than "Not Returned" – the fate of the aircraft to await definitive confirmation as and when that might be received.

The shared fate of Handley Page O/400 C9732 and its crew on the night of 20 September, 1918, is known in so far as all were brought down somewhere over the Frescaty Aerodrome on a mission to bomb and to conduct follow-up aerodrome strafing. 215 Squadron knew little of what happened to C9732 from post raid debriefs by other aircraft crews. Indeed, neither of the two aircrews who returned safely from raiding the same airfield reported either seeing C9732 go down or fire or wreckage on the ground. A squadron officer and observer, 2nd Lieutenant J. P. Armitage, who had previously flown with Fowler and considered him a "greatest pal," was able to write in a letter of condolence to next of kin only that 'ACG' had gone missing on the evening of 20 September. Armitage was actually a member of one of the two 215 Squadron aircrews to raid Frescaty successfully (twice) on the same evening of 20 September; flying over the target in Handley Page C9434[8] and an expert witness, reporting at first hand, he saw nothing that might suggest the fate of C9732. The November 1918 issue of the Hertfordshire Express reported that the Prisoner of War Agency in Switzerland had received notification from Germany that "Lieut. Fowler was brought down and killed on 21 September on the aerodrome of Fresksty (Frescaty), near Metz." The anomaly with the German date is simply explained by the raid having taken place during the dark hours comprising the evening of 20 September through the small hours of 21 September.

There were two important post scripts to Lieutenant Armitage's letter of condolence and the formal Swiss reporting of Lieutenant Fowler's shooting down. Both involve other witnesses to events. In the first, it should be noted that in 1916 after leaving Hitchin Grammar School, Fowler had become a student at the Regent Street Polytechnic, London, to study Electrical Engineering. Joining the Royal Naval Volunteer Reserve (R.N.V.R.) in June 1917, he began training as a wireless operator in the following month. This was followed by basic naval training and in December, he began basic flying training progressing to operational qualification in series of R.N.A.S. aircraft - Farman, AVRO and RAF B.E.2c (figure 11). After the war, around 5 February, 1919, a postal packet was received by Major Mitchell, Director of Education at the Regent Street Polytechnic. Apparently, the packet had been sent by a humanitarian German (identity lost) who explained that its contents, comprising a pocket book, some letters, a photograph, a Flying Corps Pilot's Certificate and a Certificate of Polytechnic Classes in Engineering, had been removed from Fowler's person after the aircraft came down. The Polytechnic Certificate provided addressing details that allowed the German to forward Fowler's personal effects, in the hope of their being subsequently redirected to his relations.   The German wrote that he had received Fowler's personal effects from a German soldier who had been at Frescaty aerodrome on the evening of 20 September. He recounted that the

---

[8] 2/Lieutenant Armitage was the observer in C9434 and the pilot was 2nd Lieutenant R.E. Kestell. Their raid on Frescaty, particularly the second on the evening of 20/21 September, 1918 verged on the heroic. In the face of "very accurate and active" searchlights and "very intense and accurate" anti-aircraft barrage, machine gun fire and 'green onions', due to strong winds, they needed to make four passes, likely all at 1,000 feet altitude, to achieve an accurate bombing run; which they did. After successfully dropping their bombs, they descended to 500 feet and strafed 'green onion' batteries. Circling at this low altitude for a half hour, they continued strafing the Frescaty. At some point, the starboard propeller was 'shot through' but C9434 was still able to recover safely to *Xaffévillers*. The take-off time for the second mission by C9434 was 23:47 and the crew would have known that Fowler's C 9732 was missing, posted 'not returned', before their departure, however, it must remain conjecture as to whether this affected how they executed their mission.

soldier explained, "Lieutenant Fowler had been sent to bombard Metz (Frescaty). I was at my post when I saw him landing (come down). At the same moment I heard a fearful explosion and when I was able to get near, I found him dead under his aeroplane."

The second involves information that was assembled after the war. Trenchard developed a number of reports in support of the value of the Royal Air Force independent bombing capability. It appears that in respect of various bombing raids, after the end of hostilities, civilians at the some target sites were interviewed to establish a clearer understanding of bombing effectiveness. Copies of these reports were found among the Trenchard papers held in the Joint Services Command and Staff College Library at Shrivenham, UK. One of these, a Department Of Intelligence Report 'On The Effects and Results of the Bombing of Germany by 8th Brigade and Independent Force, Royal Air Force: (D) Aerodromes Strategic-Tactical', records that on September 20/21, 1918, "A British aeroplane was

Figure 11: Farman (Public Domain – UK Gov. Created before 1 June 1957); AVRO (Public Domain – Iceland - Author demise (1937) plus 75 years; B.E.2C (Public Domain – Canadian Forces Image created >50 years ago)

shot down by AA fire over Frescaty and its bombs exploded on contact with the ground." The German soldier's recollection and the corroborating

Trenchard intelligence report, confirm that C9732 was brought down by enemy fire and that its remaining bombs exploded on impact. It seems likely that this was during a low-level bombing run but whether a first or second can only be guessed at. The explosive effects of the 112 lb bombs carried that night may have had surprisingly limited destructive effect above ground. Some German reports revealed that these bombs almost exclusively directed blast vertically, creating a deep crater, rather than horizontal blast damage. So, "near-misses" may have had little effect in some circumstances. This could have allowed parts of Fowler's aircraft, say the cockpit area, to remain relatively intact after bomb detonation and while the crash still proved fatal to the occupants, it would have left some personal effects relatively undamaged and available for collection by the German soldier.

Two air mechanics climbed onto the port lower wing of Handley Page C9732 and positioned themselves either side of the engine nacelle. In the cockpit, at the controls, Lieutenant Fowler signaled for the mechanics to rotate the two starting handles and the big four-bladed propeller began to turn slowly. The engine gave a dissenting kick and the Rolls-Royce Eagle VIII engine fired into life with a puff of black smoke and established rumbling idling speed. The process was repeated with the starboard engine. With both engines now idling evenly, Fowler closed off the radiator shutters and cracked the throttle open to accelerate warming up the engines. With the aircraft wheels chocked, engine operating temperatures reached and oil pressures normal, he ran-up each engine in turn to maximum revolutions on the separate magnetos to test for steady running. Satisfied with engine serviceability, he signaled for the ground crew to remove the wheel chocks. Head down, he ran his eye over the cockpit instruments (figure 27, refers) for a final check; he moved his feet, left-right, on the rudder pedals and pushed the wheel control column control backwards and forwards before rotating it left to right to ensure full range and freedom of movement of the control surfaces. C9732 was a new aircraft, just arrived and taken on squadron charge and, while he had satisfied himself of its airworthiness earlier in the day with a half-hour test flight to check it out, these final pre-flight serviceability checks would decide whether the aircraft was fit for the mission. Everything appeared sound.

The Handley Page O/400 was heavy at the controls and not agile, but Fowler was comfortable with it in the air and found that he could bring the aircraft in at extremely low altitude for bombing and strafing runs. He could fly it at one hundred feet above the ground, and he found it to be a stable, steady and safe weapon platform. His two crewmen were almost as new as Handley Page C9732 having been with the squadron for only around two-weeks. Both were observers, fresh out of training and were now being thrust straight into operations; such had become the norm across the Flying Corps because of the need to replace aircrew due to the extremely high loss rates of the Independent Force. Nevertheless, the losses were deemed to be attritionally acceptable by the Independent Force command. How would John Ferguson and Clem Eaves behave over the target? Well, he would soon find out but they seemed to be solid enough types. There was a full moon that night, so even if the course navigation was not best, with the cloud cover not too heavy, the River Moselle landmark should ensure that they would find the target. Fowler taxied C9732 carefully steering to miss any soft patches that might have resulted from the five days of driving rain earlier in September. Being heavy, carrying over 1,500 lb of bombing ordnance, he did not want the undercarriage to sink into a soft patch and the aircraft stick-in. Approaching the take-off "L", his observer, 2nd Lieutenant Eaves, flashed their aircraft number to the 'bandstand' control to request permission to take-off – 'all clear', and the bandstand flashed the same letter back in green. Turning the aircraft with a burst of port-engine throttle to position into the wind from 270, ready to go, he looked left for 2nd Lieutenant Eaves alongside him (he could not see 2nd Lieutenant Ferguson in the rear cockpit who would have to be "ready or not"). In the dimness, he saw the gauntleted thumbs up, head nodding and flash of a big smile below fur-edged goggles, which cut the darkness. Excitement rose along with the roar of the engines as the throttles were opened to full power – remaining apprehension diminishing now, swallowed by the demanding business in the cockpit and the darkness of the night. Fowler had confided to them in the operational briefing, his commitment to extreme low-level bombing and strafing runs as the only way at night to assure target accuracy, but his squadron reputation had preceded this because both knew that his average bombing height over his last eight operational missions in 215 was an extraordinary 360 feet.

Gathering speed over the grass, forward pressure on the wheel column brought the tail up; bumping now...at sustained full power, Fowler eased the control wheel back... one bump, two bumps; C9732, came unstuck, climbing sluggishly out of the airfield shadows and into the moonlight, the propeller torque (O/400 engines did not counter rotate) rolling the aircraft to starboard and requiring control wheel adjustment. Airborne and passing out of the near-ground blackness, air speed indicator showing 65 knots, climbing at a rate of 210 feet per minute, Fowler turned to starboard and out of the west onto a course three-one-five which would take them to the east of Nancy. Steadying on the course to fly, he set about synchronizing the engine speeds to remove any inclination of the aircraft to yaw. In the dark the engine exhaust manifolds were glowing cherry red, cylindrical blue flames spit from the pipe ends and, like big organ pipes, they emitted a clamoring din. He listened for the beats made by the interference between the two engine noise sources and adjusted the starboard engine to run a few RPM slower; the interval between the beats steadily increased in length as the engine speeds were equalized until the beat was completely gone. Stable and climbing, he found the Handley Page, with its few vices undemanding if sluggish to fly, thereby, leaving him with plenty of spare faculty; freeing him now to rehearse in his mind the attack on Frescaty Aerodrome. It was already feeling bone cold in the open cockpit even though he was ahead of the tearing propeller slipstream. Alongside him on his left, he was pleased to see that Eaves was engaged and working with the map on his lap; it was flapping a little as the odd eddy caught an edge as he strained to see it, illuminated with his red-filtered trench torch. Waggling his hand, towards the engines, thumb up and down in a quick turning motion, he prompted the observer to run another check on the engine-mounted temperature gauges. Yes, all well. He wondered about Ferguson, alone in the rear. Twenty minutes to crossing the lines. Toes feeling the chills but still, thank heavens for the ol' thigh-length sheepskin boots! Eaves had removed a gauntlet and rummaging in a paper bag, pulled out a boiled sweet, offering it to him – a little awkwardly with his gloved hand, he took it and popped it in his mouth; it was a humbug[9], good for moral - there would be no time for this when they crossed over the line since Frescaty was close to the front.

The mission plan called for a climb to a target altitude of 6,000 feet and to cross over enemy lines south of the recently occupied St. Mihiel Salient[10] turning east to run in over Frescaty Aerodrome, with the bend in the Moselle and the rail line to Metz staying on their left wing in the 10 o'clock position. Fowler had not flown against Frescaty Aerodrome before but the mission briefing included good overhead reconnaissance photographs, intelligence on air defenses and collateral information from other squadron aircrew who had previously made the trip. Encouragingly, the anticipated illuminating

---

[9] Traditional hard boiled sweet/candy flavoured with peppermint and striped in black-and-white colors.

[10] The St. Mihiel Salient inside the French lines had hitherto threatened communications between Nancy and the Verdun redoubt until the offensive by the American Expeditionary Force (A.E.F.) and 100,000 French troops under the command of General John J. Pershing freed the area of German occupation in an action 12-15 September, 1918.

moonlight on the 20 September would provide sufficient visibility of visual cues to allow execution of a gentle, quiet, engine-off turning descent at 60-65 mph and then a powered W-E pass over the aerodrome allowing a bomb lay-down along the near contiguous line of Frescaty aircraft sheds, buildings and hangars. The Handley Page squadrons did not fly formation at night because of the danger of collision. Aircraft mission flight times were phased to ensure airspace de-confliction although occasionally, over the target, coordination of attacks was employed as a means of decoying or confusing enemy air defenses. Since Lieutenant Buckle (D9680) and Captain Darnton (C9724) took off from Xaffévillers before his Handley Page (C9732), Fowler would have expected them to arrive ahead of him. Additionally, he would anticipate that Buckle and Darnton's night attack would have exercised the alertness of the German aerodrome defenses. Coming in as number three, he would hope that the quiet, turning dive attack and low first pass at 200-400 feet would give him some small element of surprise as the German Anti-Aircraft (AA) fire elevation would be momentarily slow to respond, although the machine gun fire would quickly find them. The return bombing and strafing runs would take their turn.

By 1918, German anti-aircraft defences had grown to be formidable. Search lights would be deployed to surround a defended area and would waft singly, lazily to and fro across the sky like a 'white stick' tap-tapping on clouds as if they sought to find by touch, intruding night raiders. Acoustic listening devices might be used to detect incoming aircraft engine noise and help direct the beam to make initial contact. Sometimes, to counter giving away their in-coming presence, raiding Handley Pages would throttle back and quietly glide down from ~6,000 feet, to arrive over the target at 1,000 – 2,000 feet, release bombs and open up the engines and power away; power-on being determined by when the element of surprise was lost. If one searchlight found an aircraft, others would snap to follow and quickly try to lock on to it too. The light was dazzling making the aircraft shimmer, every edge clear cut with every feature flood-lit from below; illuminated such that upper surfaces were shadowed in deepest, black contrasting relief. Aircrew might be disorientated and blinded and, still worse, anti-aircraft artillery batteries within a wide radius of the target would be drawn to moth-like illuminated targets, opening fire, cued now to bring them down. An aircraft caught in a beam would take immediate evasive action to break the searchlight director's lock; any hesitation might allow additional beams to follow and compound the problem and make escape more difficult. A technique to break beam lock was to begin by making a steep turn to dive down the beam and, thereby, present the smallest cross section to the searchlight director. Gathering speed, the aircraft might then be side-slipped to port or starboard or pulled up into a stall turn to slide out from the beam now coming from astern. In the normal course, aerobatics were forbidden as unsafe in the ponderous Handley Page O/400 but the searchlight evasion technique was reported effective even though the aircraft air speed might exceed 100 mph.

For close-in defence, the German 3.7 cm Maschinenkanone Flak[11] (3.7 cm M-Flak) was a capable machine gun. It could be mounted on a rotating pedestal with a gunner's seat and a large box or drum which held a hundred-round cloth belt. It fired around 250 rounds per minute. The effective ceiling was probably a little in excess of 1,000 m (3,250 ft) although the flat range was 4,000 m (13,000 ft). Although it was without a fire-control system, it had proved to be effective when positioned behind the lines to provide defence against low-flying trench-strafing British and French aircraft. It could fire Hotchkiss ball and tracer shells that traced bright green at night and enabled the gunner to "hose" rounds at an enemy aircraft.

The 8.8 cm Flak 16 was a German 88 mm anti-aircraft (AA) artillery gun and was introduced in 1917, superseding the less capable 7.7 cm Flak gun. Mounted on a lorry, it was mobile and it was designed to be bespoke to anti-aircraft defence having a high muzzle velocity. It was well able to engage Handley Page O/400 aircraft up to their operational altitude ceiling. Most AA shells produced fragments to maximize dispersion, but high-explosive and incendiary shells were also used. By 1917, mechanical fuses had entered service that enabled round detonation after a preset flight time, set to equate to the estimated altitude of aircraft operation. AA guns might be located on a defensive perimeter, a mile or more from a defended point and provide a wide area air-defensive screen through which an attacking aircraft would have to pass. For British airmen, anti-aircraft fires were sometimes referred to by the slang terms of "Archie or "Ack-Ack fire."[12] At night, AA high-explosive rounds bursting in the sky about an aircraft would be seen as bright red flashes resembling shooting stars or if closer, as bursts of 'red sparks' that lived momentarily and then quickly faded-out but left behind, unseen, an

---

[11] Flak is a contraction of the German 'Flugzeugabwehrkanone' meaning "aircraft-defense cannon."

[12] Archie was the collective term for anti-aircraft guns and fires. It is reputed that the term came from a British pilot who responded to whether he had been hit by enemy anti-aircraft fire by recounting the line from a music hall song 'Archibald certainly not'. Additionally, in the British phonetic alphabet, developed with the use of radio-telephones, 'A' was articulated as 'Ack' and so, 'anti-aircraft' would be referred to as 'Ack–Ack.'

expanding 'bubble' of black shrapnel, whizzing inaudibly, drowned by engine noise. Colloquially, the accuracy of AA might be attributed three levels of concern by aircrew under fire: 'a red flash – near enough to demand your attention; over the din of the engines and wind noise, a dull 'woof' – near enough to take evasive action; a sharp crack - lucky if you were still there to take action!'

Lastly, anti-aircraft fires known by the sobriquet 'flaming green onions' (FGO) caused aircrews some alarm early on in the air war. To the aircrews, flying at night, FGOs appeared to be like a string of green glowing balls which followed each other, in line, initially languid, curving in their upward flight like joined living things that then seemed to chase an aircraft,

Figure 12: 8: 37 mm Gruson-Hotchkiss Revolverkanone revolving-barrel anti-aircraft gun that fired the strings of 'flaming green onions' reported by the night bomber Handley Page O-type crews (courtesy of the Brett Butterworth collection)

accelerating in an arc towards it. Actually, the flaming onion was a low velocity flare that was fired by a 37 mm *Gruson-Hotchkiss Revolverkanone*, revolving-barrel anti-aircraft gun, designed to fire multiple projectiles in rapid order over a defensive area. The gun (figure 12) was a 'Gatling' type, smooth bore, revolving short barreled automatic that the Germans nicknamed, '*lichtspucker*' (light-spitter). Each of the gun's five barrels could launch a 37 mm artillery shell to around five thousand feet and, to maximize the chance of hitting an aircraft, all five rounds were discharged as rapidly as possible, giving the 'string of flaming onions' effect – the green flame color resulted from the use of barium salts in the shell charges. Most other anti-aircraft artillery at the time fired relatively slowly but the 37 mm gun, with either five or ten-round feed trays put several shells in the air simultaneously leaving British aircrew with the impression that the rounds were attached to a flailing string, which they feared might slice through the aircraft. Ironically, the weapon was not designed as an anti-aircraft weapon since the shell was a non-explosive flare, however, with a direct hit on a fabric-covered aircraft, it might have ignited a fire. Adapted for anti-aircraft defence, it appears that its principal effectiveness was to cause an attacking aircraft to manoeuver evasively and thereby to disrupt an attack run. As part of a defensive strategy this value should not be underestimated since facing the unknown usually denies the employment of good countermeasures. The FGO artillery remained a mystery to allied aircrews because they were located at defensive positions behind the lines and none were captured until late in the war. As a result, Flaming Green Onions remained a somewhat disconcerting 'secret weapon', "putting the wind up" some aircrews until the end of hostilities on the Western Front. Their 'green balls' epithet became the stuff of legend for British aircrews and the title of one book on WW1 Handley Page bombers, in particular[13].

Now passing over the industrial centre of Nancy to their west and further to the north the former German occupied St. Mihiel Salient, that days before was captured by 'Black Jack' Pershing and his American-French ground and allied air forces, Handley Page O/400 C9732 was challenged "friend or foe" by a pencil thin light that flashed '— · —'... 'K' in Morse code. Eaves quickly fired the loaded Very pistol through the cockpit floor steel tube receptacle and the red-white flare fell away to secure safe passage through the airspace from allied anti-air artillery fire. All quiet now with the enemy lines ahead. 2nd Lieutenant Fowler, 'Garrie' to his family and known as 'ACG' in the squadron, was nineteen years old and was flying the largest British warplane of that time. Captain of the aircraft and flying into action, he carried a level of responsibility that was thoroughly awesome for a young man of nineteen years; there must have been moments when he felt extreme pride. Undoubtedly living on frayed nerves, perhaps he doubted high command's appreciation of his work in the air. Repeated exposure to combat and the corrosive effect of extreme losses would have caused inevitable doubts. Nevertheless, this evening, piloting C9732, he evidentially

---

[13] "Green Balls, the Adventures of a Night Bomber" by Paul Bewsher, William Blackwood and Sons, Edinburgh and London, 1919.

understood his duty and his responsibility to his companions and 215 Squadron. To achieve best military effectiveness, he knew very clearly that he had to run in low over the target to achieve definitive identification and bombing accuracy. This called for extreme daring – he had demonstrated this not once but many times during his period of operations, from late August through to this evening of 20th September. Anti-aircraft fires - the crack of a nearby exploding shell would be heard over the scream of the engines and the air percussion snapped taut the canvas on the fuselage sides, in and out like a drum skin. Machine-gun tracer would search serpent-like for the aircraft and flaming green onions would rise and bend towards the aircraft as though attracted to a mythological Siren. And the air would reek with the swirling odorous wafts of burnt amatol[14] high explosive, whose smell was sharply acrid and similar to burned hair and which made aircrew "gasp for breath." Eaves, his observer, was operationally inexperienced but had that quality of resilience that comes with excitement and being fresh to the fight; it was so different with his usual left-hander, Preedy, who was absent this evening having sought respite to repair his frayed nerves. Still climbing at a rate of around 220 feet per minute and with the lines around 45 miles from Xaffévillers, Handley Page O/400 C9732 probably crossed over the German lines at a little under 4,500 feet, almost certainly without incident.

From this point onwards, 2nd Lieutenant Fowler's final flight becomes more uncertain. Captain Darnton's C9724 had launched eighteen minutes before Fowler's C9732 and most likely attacked Frescaty before C9732's arrival and thereby alerted anti-aircraft air defences over the aerodrome and also the AA batteries at Metz, around five miles to the north. There is little doubt that the Frescaty/Metz-Sablon area was well defended with anti-aircraft defences (including Jagdstaffel aircraft) at this time, witness 99 Squadron's 26 September loss of five aircraft constituting fifty percent of the attacking aircraft. On the night of 20/21 September, later raid intelligence debriefs reported that searchlights were on target and that anti-aircraft activity was intense and heavy in a wide radius of the Frescaty target. Leaving Xaffévillers, Eaves would probably have set a course of around three-one-five taking into account a westerly wind that was to freshen significantly after 23:00. It likely gave him a relative flight course of three-four-zero

---

[14] Amatol/Füllpulver (German), is a highly explosive material made from a mixture of trinitrotoluene (TNT) (C_6H_2-CH_3-$(NO_2)_3$) and ammonium nitrate (NH_4NO_3). The German Army, during WW1, used it in the mixture composed by 60% T.N.T., and 40% ammonium nitrate as Füllpulver 60/40. It was used extensively in military weapons as the bursting charge for shells, bombs and depth charges.

(figure 13). Dead reckoning would have allowed him to anticipate time of crossing the lines, which on a clear night would have been distinct and a good navigation cueing or way point. Staying on his course bearing for around a further five to eight minutes would bring the aircraft a little to the west of Frescaty, well positioned to begin a descending turn to the right to attack in a W-E run. If C9732 overshot making the turn to starboard, the River Moselle and railway line to its north would have provided obvious landmarks to highlight missing the turn. Although night visibility was good with the full moon, ground geography from 4000 feet altitude, made less distinct by a number of shadowed forest copses, would have made identification of 'blacked-out' Frescaty aerodrome somewhat ambiguous initially. However, once determined, the contiguous line of aircraft hangars,

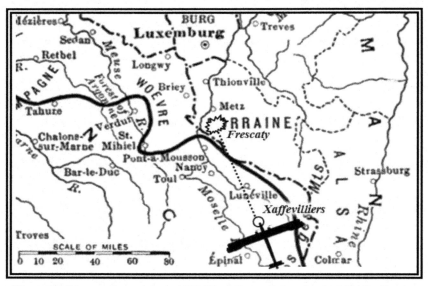

Figure 13: Western Front August 1918 (black line and showing St. Mihiel salient) – Xaffévillers/ Frescaty Aerodromes (Public Domain - Prior 1 January, 1923

Casino de Frescaty and aircraft sheds on the north east side of the aerodrome would have provided actionable points of reference.

It seems quite likely that Fowler made a straight-in attack, despite not having bombed Frescaty before. He may have made an engine-off descent to mask C9732's arrival at the aerodrome and this probably began at four to five miles out; the Handley Page rate of descent, engines off, was around 1,000 feet per ground mile covered. As soon as he was caught in the Frescaty searchlights, banking on the engines not having cooled down too much, to miss a beat, Fowler would have opened the throttles and run up the Rolls-Royce Eagle VIIIs. The German soldier who witnessed C9732 brought down indicated that there had been a "fearful" explosion when the aircraft impacted with the ground; he also indicated that he had been close to the event, suggesting that the aircraft was making a very low-level pass. While rupturing fuel tanks and subsequent fuel atomization alone would have certainly have provided the constituents of an explosive effect, there is the strongest suggestion that some aircraft bombs on board the aircraft also exploded. The German was apparently also quickly on the scene of the wreck but wrote that he was delayed in approaching, most likely because there was fire or further danger of other ordnance detonating. That he was subsequently able to find Fowler's body below the aircraft with note-books and personal effects intact, suggests that the aircraft nose was blown forward in the melee of the crash. The eye-witnessed explosion supports an understanding that 2nd Lieutenant Fowler was engaged in a bombing and not a strafing run when he was hit and brought down by enemy fire. Whether he was brought down on a first or second or even later run over the target must be left to conjecture (unless a later written witness to the action emerges with finer recollection). Certainly, the freshening westerly wind after midnight caused aiming problems for 2nd Lieutenant R. E. Kestell's C9434, when making S to N bombing runs, and he reported that he was obliged to fly "over the target four times…in order to get good shooting" (a euphemism for bombs on target). As noted earlier, the Mk. I High Altitude Drift Sight effectiveness was markedly degraded if used in anything but headwind conditions. Kestell's bombing runs were flown at 1,000 feet altitude and he attacked facilities to the south and to the north east of the aerodrome. The best existing photographs of the time (aerial and otherwise) show little distinct evidence of hangars on the southern perimeter but certainly, there were various AA emplacements and searchlights. Kestell took credit for direct bombing hits on the permanent hangars and chateau (fort) lying on the contiguous NW to SE line along the aerodrome's northern margin. Based on his previous bombing raids and consistent with his reputation for daring low-level bombing that had been established within the squadron,[15] it is likely

---

[15] No. 215 Handley Page Night Bombing Squadron, Royal Air Force History makes special mention of Fowler, as follows: "2/LIEUT. A.C.G FOWLER. Born: June 1889. Was commissioned in the R.N.A.S. 28th Oct. 1917. Joined this Squadron July 1918 and was responsible for many excellent low bombing raids; his average height from which he bombed upon eight consecutive occasions was 360'. While carrying out a raid on FRESCATY AERODROME, he was shot down; buried at METZ GARRISON CEMETARY." While Fowler was not awarded a decoration in recognition of his daring low level raids,

that Fowler bombed Frescaty Aerodrome on the evening of 20 September from very low altitude. He probably attacked from W to E because the line of northern permanent facilities was most visually detectible at night and he cued his attack to begin by bombing the imposing Zeppelin hangar that book-ended the target-line to the west. Numerous searchlights were very active criss-crossing the darkness of the sky. They were reported by other crews that night, to be accurately directed whether prompted by following engine noise detection or director's intuition, it is not known. FGO batteries, AA barrage and machine guns too, were accurately directed that night and Kestell notes that in his second raid, his propeller was "shot through" - probably by machine-gun fire.

Six minutes flying time after crossing the lines to the south of the St. Mihiel Salient and responding to observer Eaves' direction, Fowler turned Handley Page C9732 for a new course one-one-zero. He applied right rudder first and, as the aircraft began to slowly yaw to starboard, he turned the column wheel clockwise to roll the heavy aircraft and to enter a gentle, if delayed, turn; as the compass head came round, taking off control inputs, he centered up on the new course without overshoot. Before the turn, Eaves had sighted the River Moselle to the NE and believed that the target, Frescaty aerodrome, should lie seven miles ahead along the new bearing. Peering into the dark shadows and reflected moonshine from clear ground that sheened off sharp-edged reflectors like roadways and buildings, Fowler and Eaves strained to locate the aerodrome. Fowler cut the engines and they were descending now through 4,000 feet and four miles out by eye. The quiet was still disturbed by the wind ripping around the cockpit combing and some bracing wires were singing quietly; nevertheless, the general silence was eerie with the moonlight giving the upper aircraft surfaces a spectral gleam but with the lower surfaces remaining caught in deep and cloying black shadow. Eaves slipped forward to the bomb aiming Drift Sight and gave thumbs up that he was ready to go. Fowler worried that he had cut the engines too soon since altitude was important when discriminating grass strip airfields from open farmland. Three miles... altitude 2,300 feet....he and Eaves, the second pointing vigorously, saw the big Zeppelin hangar

---

which were quite extraordinary, the letter of condolence to next-of-kin by his squadron friend 2nd Lieutenant J.P. Armitage notes that he had been recommended for a gallantry award but, the action would have been terminated with his death because other than the Victoria Cross, recognitions were not usually made posthumously. However, Armitage writes that he was mentioned in dispatches twice. Further, Armitage wrote that, Fowler, "as a pilot he was superb and was among the best that I ever had the pleasure to fly with as an observer." Finally, Armitage sums up his friend who he and the squadron called "ACG", as "a brave aviator and a gentleman."

simultaneously. Concurrently, multiple searchlights from ahead and to the right lit up and began to sweep across the sky. How long before the aircraft was caught in a beam? – He needed power to side-slip. The engines were still warm and to his relief, ran up quickly, roaring in unison. Caught in the stroke of a beam, he instinctively closed his eyes momentarily and quickly side-slipped C9732 right and diving, he lost the beam but he had little altitude to spare and was flying fast. The anti-aircraft barrage had opened up but the red bursts were astern of the aircraft. Green onion[16] strings appeared to their left but were two or three miles abeam. Of greater concern was the machine gun fire that formed a curtain of green in a wide radius of the hangar and that now evidently extended along the line of the other buildings. They would bomb by eye. At three hundred feet, skimming the Zeppelin hangar, Fowler released ten 112 lb bombs, sequentially along the line of the permanent structures, including the Casino de Frescaty and aircraft sheds. Pulling up and to the right, first one, and then a second searchlight picked the aircraft out of the night. AA fires and tracer from the aerodrome southern barrage raked the aircraft, it staggered in the air…it came wings-level, descending flatly onto the airfield, breaking up and then at least one of the four remaining bombs exploded[17].

It is quite possible that 2nd Lieutenant Fowler was hit by machine gun fire or AA shrapnel and that, wounded, he exerted control over the aircraft in a desperate attempt to level it and crash land. This appears to be consistent with the German soldier's enigmatic description of how the aircraft was brought down, saying, "standing at my post, I saw him landing." The use of the word 'landing' in English implies a controlled event and in this case appears out of place for an impact that ended with the aircraft breaking up. The sense may have been corrupted in the translation from German – for example, *'Bruchlandung'* is a German word for the English 'crash landing' and in translation, simply, *'Landung'* may have been preserved as the principal descriptive term, resulting in the direct employment of the English

---

[16] Despite their unsettling appearance, in his book "The Big Bombers of World War I" Lieutenant Hugh Monaghan notes that "Only one case was known of our planes running into them. An F.E. 2b returned one night with a long strand of copper wire trailing from its wing. Attached to the wire were two tufts of charred metal."

[17] The blast effect of a 112 lb bomb may have been relatively limited, particularly if buried during the crash. Principally designed to generate fragments with high kinetic energy, cratering may have been limited to a hole five feet deep by fifteen feet across and parts of C9432 may have been relatively unscathed by the blast (e.g. tail, nose, outer wings…) with main damage due to impact with the ground and, catching fire.

word, 'landing'. That 2nd Lieutenants Fowler, Eaves and Ferguson perished in the crash is beyond doubt. The Great War was entering its final phase but the three airmen were given a military funeral and buried in the Metz Garrison graveyard. The German soldier who was on hand at the crash found Fowler's body under the nose and was able to recover notebook and personal effects that later found their way back to next of kin.

Back in Xaffévillers, it was 04:15 on the morning of 21 September. The 215 Squadron Intelligence Officer had finished debriefing the Kestell C9434 crew after their second mission of the night and after they had recovered safely to Xaffévillers at 02:15. Their half-hour strafing of Frescaty Aerodrome had been very, very aggressive and he knew that the observer, Armitage, had been close to Fowler. Perhaps Armitage would write to family if necessary – well, that was getting ahead of things and, besides, it was for the boss, Major Jones to suggest, if indeed the worst had happened. Leafing through the After-Action debrief report forms, he withdrew the open page headed "Frescaty, 20/21 Sept 1918, C9732" with the names Fowler, Eaves and Ferguson below. In pencil - he invariably wrote the intelligence debriefs in pencil with a rubber (eraser) close by to delete mistakes or immediate reconsiderations - in lower case, he wrote, "not returned", striking lines above and below as if to reduce how bleak these two words appeared on the blank page. What was the chance that "A.C.G" and the two new boys had force landed...well, he'd hope for the best and time would provide the truth of it?

Epilogue

The story of the Royal Air Force (R.A.F) began a little over one hundred years ago on 1 April, 1918. No. 215 Squadron, Independent Force (IF) was formed at the same time (Appendix K refers). Leaving behind his Royal Naval Air Service (R.N.A.S.) beginnings, 2nd Lieutenant A.C.G. Fowler joined 215 in the newly established R.A.F service on 7 July, 1918, just twenty days after his nineteenth birthday. He flew operationally during the months August and September 1918 coinciding with the final stages of World War 1. Along with his two Handley Page O/400 crew companions, he was most likely brought down by enemy fire over Frescaty Aerodrome on 20 September. In that short period of operations, he established himself as a distinguished squadron pilot; skillful in the air, daring and committed to the service of his country.

Figure 14: Major-General Hugh Trenchard, Commander Independent Force, June-Dec 1918 (© IWM Q 2536)

In the final instance, most military men and women do not think of glory, they think of life - but society in 1918, changing, but rooted still in the fading nostalgia of the Victorian century was less complicated in the way that it eulogized those sons and daughters who bore the heaviest burden. Most schooled British young men at that time would have been familiar with Lord Macaulay's poem which has Horatius announcing, "... And how can man die better, than facing fearful odds". Well, Fowler and his crew, his 215 Squadron colleagues and indeed, the whole Independent Force, certainly did face 'fearful odds'; witness the massive losses that they sustained. As men they would have displayed modesty and would likely have eschewed the grand title of heroes only too aware of their fears under fire that later visited them in quiet, dark moments. But, today, it is we who are their judges not they, and their facing 'fearful odds', again and again and returning to the fight is a measure that unequivocally defines them as the bravest of men. Yet, Macaulay's other words, "how can a man die better" suggests a second consideration which is exclusive of any courage demanded of the aircrews contesting a metaphorical Pons Sublicius[18]. Given the stakes, the Independent Force impact on enemy capability (military and civil) needed to be worth the cost in lives and lost material and, to assess this; we scrutinize today, the Commander's decisions and mindset. Major-General Trenchard (figure 14) was the commander of note and it was he who made the raiding policy and it is he who must be judged on the heavy losses and whether his calculus for strategic bombing was *value added* and, therefore, justified.

Trenchard's Independent Force command had aspects of being a private air force. Some of the politics regarding his appointment have been mentioned in the foregoing, as has his evident personal courage, reflected in his military record as a young man during the Boer War. Less complimentary, was his failure to appreciate the nuanced challenges of developing air warfare, the technology limitations of the aircraft and the need to weigh military achievement against losses rather than to drive his squadrons forward in a wasteful, attritional manner. While his Independent Force remit was strategic bombing, to which he was personally antipathetic, he channeled the force into tactical bombing. Smarter tactical commanders seek to conserve resources but Trenchard, a man of the old imperium and less of science, poured machines and new crews into the fight despite the growing erosion of their warfighting preparedness and the

Figure 15: Second Lieutenant Roy Shillinglaw, No. 100 Squadron, 1918 – who died aged 100 years on 24 September 1999 in the Isle of Man

---

[18] For the curious - Pons Sublicius was the bridge over the Tiber that Macaulay's Horatius and his two companions, Spurius Lartius and Herminius, defended against the invading army of Lars Porsena, King of Clusium in the 6th century BC

critical dilution of the experience pool. There appear aspects of Trenchard's Independent Force all-out charge into bombing operations that seem to echo another desperate charge - the one that took place at Balaklava in 1855.

His personal approach is illustrated in a recollection by 2nd Lieutenant Roy Shillinglaw (figure 15) of 100 Squadron. 100 Squadron, Independent Force, had given up their FE.2Bs for Handley Page O/400s and in one of their first flights, an aircraft took-off complete with an ordnance load, only to stall and crash. Eight squadron personnel ran over to try to rescue the aircrew but the bombs exploded, killing all eight and the aircrew. Shillinglaw wrote that next day; Lord Trenchard visited the squadron and made a speech to the squadron officers. He recounted that Trenchard 'sat on his stick and in repose' he said, "Gather round…It's very unfortunate, just getting a new machine and this happens" ("…and this, that and the other", Shillinglaw extemporizes). "But nevertheless, there are plenty more pilots, plenty more observers and plenty more machines in the pool. Get cracking! My targets have got to be bombed!" Shillinglaw writes, "That's all he said and that was that. I heard him say that myself" - sardonically, Shillinglaw opines how hugely morale boosting was the General's speech.

The losses of the Independent Force were unsustainable had not the Armistice been signed in early November 1918 and bombing missions ceased. Between June and November 1918, sources[19] report that 109 bombers of the Independent Force were lost over enemy territory and 243 more aircraft crashed ('wastage') for a variety of reasons over allied territory (making a total loss of 352 aircraft). During September 1918, seventy-five percent of the Independent Force material establishment was lost in action. Statistically, it was suggested that it took the loss of around five British aircraft to destroy one German aircraft on the ground and on average; one Independent Force aircraft was lost every three raids and one aircraft for every 1.54 tons of bombs dropped. Undoubtedly, it was Trenchard's offensive policy that resulted in the high losses between June and November 1918 – he alone was architect of the policy. Of the four daytime Independent Force squadrons, only 55 Squadron operated without interruption despite losses of 125 percent of overall squadron strength during the period. 99, 104 and 110 were forced recurrently to suspend operations. Of the night squadrons, as has been noted, 215 Squadron sustained 120 percent losses. There is little sense that Trenchard troubled himself with the science of

---

[19] H.A. Jones, The War in the Air (23), 'Statistics of Work of Squadrons of the Independent Force, Including Wastage, June-November 1918'

military cost effectiveness for either material or lives lost. Even though personally the executor, entrusted with the military employment of the Independent Force, Trenchard was to write on 11 November, 1918, "The Armistice was signed this morning. Thus the Independent Force comes to an end. A more gigantic waste of effort and personnel there never has been in any war."[20] Whatever his dissatisfactions with the Independent Force, this expression suggests doubts that are thoroughly inconsistent with ordering the men under his command on offensive missions for little material gain. It is hard to escape drawing a conclusion that Trenchard took a callous view of the losses.

Why "rake over old coals", is it really necessary? After all Lord Trenchard is viewed by some as the father of the Royal Air Force with buildings and institutions named after him and, undoubtedly, he did much to preserve the fledgling Air Force's independence. In the centenary year, questioning him may add some tarnish to celebrating the great Service that Royal Air Force has become. Well, the answer is still, 'yes, very much so; start rummaging those coals with the poker.' The real heroes are the aircrew of C9732, other Handley Page O/400 crews and their DH 4/9/9A comrades of the Independent Force; both day and night squadrons. They come out of this story, blemish free. They contended with enemy fire and also the impossibilities that their own command required of them. Simply, men such as 2/Lieutenant A.C.G. Fowler did their duty in the face of 'fearful odds.' Theirs was just one armed rehearsal for the later defining moment of the Royal Air Force when, in those same months August and September but in 1940, the Luftwaffe launched its systematic assault on Fighter Command; perhaps more enigmatically were seeds sown leading to the later R.A.F. WW II area-bombing policy. In the best moment, its airmen became legendary by winning the sobriquet, "the Few." For this family, for whom Garrie was the great and now great-great uncle who did not return, there has grown a feeling of immense pride for the fine young man revealed in the archived reports, operational orders, post-mission intelligence debriefs and a patchwork of other histories. Undoubtedly, he was a young 'Horatius at the Bridge' with his two brave companions and it is the duty done in August and September 1918 that brings the truest credit to the R.A.F. today. And for the future, surely, beyond argument, families have a right to expect that the lives of their sons and daughters be shed parsimoniously by their Commanders, flying good missions based on the best intelligence and for good cause.

---

[20] Trenchard's private diary, 11 November, 1918 (unsighted).

Appendix A

Second Lieutenant A.C.G. Fowler, RAF 215 Squadron - Mission Record for the Period 6 August – 20 September, 1918 (from: Mission reports accessed at the National Archives, Kew, UK, February 2017)

Date /1918	Aircrew Observer G/L = gunlayer	Target	Time Out/ Time Rtn	HP O/400 Aircraft #	Details from 215 Squadron Mission Reports
6/7 Aug	Pilot Buck* Obs Barter G/L Fowler Passenger Sprague	Railway Axe between Blanche Maison and Douai	10.43/12.55	D9683	Dropped 16 x 112 lb 10 x 25 lb bombs at 11.30 at 500 ft **SAA fired No. of rounds:** 700 **Targets:** Searchlights either side of railway N of Douai, Town of Henin Lietard at 1000 ft **DETAILS OF ATTACK:** Took N course from Douai, attacked line at about W4. Dropped bombs in one long straddle along the lines. Observed bursts but no direct hits claimed. Visibility fair. Good shooting made. **OBSERVATIONS:** From Douai to Lens. Flares were lit at intervals from the ground as machine passed over at 500 to 1000 ft possibly to show Hun scouts positions of machine. **EA Activity:** **AA Activity:** heavy, fairly accurate **Searchlights:** Big, active **Flaming Onions:** Carvin
9/10 Aug	Pilot Buck* Obs Barter G/L Preedy Passenger Fowler	Cambrai	12.40/1.45	D9863	Port engine failure Landed with bombs intact Visibility impossible **DETAILS OF ATTACK:** Proceeded Eauluns so returned owing to Port Engine failure and landed back with bombs intact
10/11 Aug	Pilot Buck* Obs Barter G/L Fowler	Cambrai Gare Annexe	9.20/12.20	D9863	Dropped 16 x 112 lb bombs, 10 x 25 lb bombs at 10.40 at 6000 ft **SAA fired No. of rounds:** 650 **Targets:** Searchlights Sailly Marquoin Arras rd **DETAILS OF ATTACK:** Approached NW to SE Dropped in one run 4/112 on town

Date /1918	Aircrew Observer G/L = gunlayer	Target	Time Out/ Time Rtn	HP O/400 Aircraft #	Details from 215 Squadron Mission Reports
					12/112 in line N Gare Annexe Bursts observed 14/25 in vicinity (Searchlight extinguished) Visibility fair **OBSERVATIONS:** Red T at Estourmel 6000 ft seen from Cambrai **EA Activity:** (light only seen) hovering over town 5500! 10.40 Fire at 10.45 N of Marquoin (Cambrai) Tracer fired from air W of Cambrai **AA Activity:** Nil **Searchlights:** Four active Cambrai Baupaume Rd accurate **Flaming onions:** Active Merquies accurate
11 Aug	Pilot Lawson Obs Towill G/L Fowler	Cambrai (SE) Rly Station	9.23/12.08	C9658	Dropped 16 x 112 lb, 14 x 25 lb bombs at 10.55 at 4000 ft Visibility fair **SAA fired No. of rounds:** 1500 **Targets:** Searchlights on Cambrai Arras Road Lights red and green on ground at Tilloy extinguished **DETAILS OF ATTACK:** took run from SE to NW of Railway Station (Gare annexe) Dropped 16/112 in one salvo well straddling the target Bursts observed and 4 bombs seen to explode in sidings. 14/25 on Town and Station in a run from E to W Bursts observed **OBSERVATIONS:** Lights 2 white 100 yards apart Epinoy and Harfuecourt-Epinoy 11.40 Fired at and extinguished S. Onions Le Calean [Chateau] 1 gap 3 Cambrai 10.25-11.00 2 Fires Henin Lietard 10.20 to 11.15 from Arras-Cambrai Rd Searchlights (7 or 8) Dury Arras Cambrai Rd Considerable activity in Gare Annexe. Lights extinguished when machine glided over **EA Activity:** Nil

Date /1918	Aircrew Observer G/L = gunlayer	Target	Time Out/ Time Rtn	HP O/400 Aircraft #	Details from 215 Squadron Mission Reports
					AA Activity: light inaccurate **Searchlights:** Active Very accurate **Flaming Onions:** Direct hits 4/112
12 Aug	Pilot Buck* Obs Barter G/L Fowler	Cut off	9.20/11.50	D9863	Dropped 16 x 112 lb bombs, 10 x 25 lb bombs at 10.50 pm at 6000 ft **SAA fired No. of rounds:** 1000 **Targets:** Red flares and lights at Recourt and lights on Arras Cambrai Rd **DETAILS OF ATTACK:** Dropped 16/112 10/25 bombs in vicinity of Bugnicourt Bursts unobserved due to very low visibility (thick mist / fog) **OBSERVATIONS:** Nil **EA activity:** Nil **AA activity:** Nil **Searchlights:** Nil **Flaming onions:** Nil
13 Aug	Pilot Buck Obs Barter G/L Fowler	Cambrai Gare Annexe	9.36/12.05	D9863	Dropped 16 x 112 lb, 10 x 25 lb bombs at 10.47 at 6000 ft **SAA fired No. of rounds:** 1300 **Targets:** Searchlights Arras Cambrai **DETAILS OF ATTACK:** Dropped 12/112 in line from N to S Bursts observed on Cambrai Gare Annexe sidings and lines and all direct hits claimed 4/112 dropped just N of Cambrai G.A. Station Bursts observed Visibility good 10/25 dropped in final run **OBSERVATIONS:** One HP dropping at 10.45 over target **EA activity:** Nil **AA activity:** Active and intense at the machines **Searchlights:** Active as well **Flaming onions:** Fairly active
14 Aug	Pilot Fowler Obs Preedy G/L Sprague	Cambrai Gare Annexe	9.58/12.56	D4568	Dropped 14 x 112 lb, 9 x 25 lb bombs at 11.20 at 6000 ft **SAA fired No. of rounds:** 1400

Date /1918	Aircrew Observer G/L = gunlayer	Target	Time Out/ Time Rtn	HP O/400 Aircraft #	Details from 215 Squadron Mission Reports
					Targets: Searchlights Arras Cambrai Monquison Sailly **DETAILS OF ATTACK:** 14/112 lb in vicinity of station and sidings in one run from SE to NW Bursts observed 9/25 dropped on line toward N of station Bursts observed Good shooting Visibility good **OBSERVATIONS:** Fire at Cambrai still burning Douai onions ---of 4 S.O. S Baupaume 11.45 Cambrai Baupaume Rd **EA activity:** Nil **AA activity:** Active S of Arras Cambrai **Searchlights:** Very active and accurate **Flaming onions:** Nil
15 Aug	Pilot Lawson Obs Towill G/L Fowler	Cambrai Gare Annexe	9.22/11.30	C9658	Dropped 16 x 112 lb, 10 x 25 lb bombs at 10.30 at 3000 ft **SAA fired No. of rounds:** Nil **Targets:** ---- **DETAILS OF ATTACK:** Bombs dropped on Dury Bursts observed through undercloud Visibility very poor **OBSERVATIONS:** Douai onions Lights coming through the clouds **EA activity:** Nil **AA activity:** **Searchlights:** **Flaming onions:**
22 Aug	Pilot Fowler Obs Preedy G/L Sprague	Folperweiler	8.30/12.00	D4568	Dropped 16 x 112 lb bombs, 10 x 25 lb bombs at 11.16 at 3000 ft **SAA fired No. of rounds:** 600 **Targets:** Aerodrome **DETAILS OF ATTACK:** Approached from NE 4/112 dropped in S corner Bursts observed and direct hits one hutments claimed. Small fire started to W of aerodrome just W of hutments. Several big fires observed in W corner of aerodrome and explosions seen

Date /1918	Aircrew Observer G/L = gunlayer	Target	Time Out/ Time Rtn	HP O/400 Aircraft #	Details from 215 Squadron Mission Reports
					OBSERVATIONS: 4/112 to S of fire 8/112 in close proximity to hangars in N corner of aerodrome 10/25 dropped on run from SE to NW areas W end of aerodrome Transport active near scene of fire Lights from ---- same side SW Saabrucken **EA activity:** 12 EA dropping on Lieuville 9.30 6000/7000 **AA activity:** Light and inaccurate **Searchlights:** Light and inaccurate **Flaming onions:** Nil
23 Aug	Pilot Fowler Obs Preedy G/L Sprange	Boulay	7.55/11.20	D4568	Dropped 16 x 112 lb bombs 10 x 25 lb bombs at 9.35 at 3000 ft **SAA fired No. of rounds:** 400 **Targets:** Searchlights, hutments hangars and landing T on aerodrome **DETAILS OF ATTACK:** 16/112 and 10/25 dropped on line of hangars from SE to NW of aerodrome. Some bursts observed some unobserved with glare of searchlights but at target for half an hour. Searchlights and AA barrage Kept machine at bay. Visibility fair over target Storm encountered on homeward course and m/c landed in thunderstorm **OBSERVATIONS:** Landing L observed to E of Metz 9.10 Signalling onions groups of 3 at erratic intervals in vicinity of Monseon **EA activity:** 1 EA seen preparing to land on aerodrome **AA activity:** Heavy in vicinity of target Accurate **Searchlights:** Accurate active Bionville aerodrome **Flaming onions:** Active E of Metz
25 Aug	Pilot Fowler Obs Preedy G/L Sprague	Boulay	7.55/11.50	D4568	Dropped 16 x 112 lb 11 x 25 lb at 9.26 at 1500 ft **SAA fired No. of rounds:** 1400

Date /1918	Aircrew Observer G/L = gunlayer	Target	Time Out/ Time Rtn	HP O/400 Aircraft #	Details from 215 Squadron Mission Reports
					Targets: Searchlights on aerodrome and in vicinity hutments + hangars on aerodrome **DETAILS OF ATTACK:** Approached target from SE and took one run over line of hangars running from ESE to WNW Bombs were dropped in close proximity to hangars on aerodrome Some bursts observed but were not seen owing to intense AA barrage and extreme and accurate activity of searchlights Believe good marksmanship obtained M/C remained over target sweeping the aerodrome with MG fire Visibility was fairly good except for occasional low clouds **OBSERVATIONS:** Landing L SE Metz seen 9.10 2 m/cs observed on ground with navigation lights on To W of Boulay Landing L and lights fired presumably during aerodrome--- NNW Boulay Green and red lights flashing at erratic intervals "D" Lighthouse not working 10 SO **EA activity:** Nil Gotha bombing Xaffévillers **AA activity:** Very heavy (over) target **Searchlights:** Very heavy (over) target **Flaming onions:** Very heavy (over) target
30 Aug	Pilot Fowler Obs Preedy G/L Fisher + Harrison	Boulay	7.50/11.10	D4568	Dropped 16 x 112 lb bombs (Noted they were "Hung up") 10 x 25 lb bombs at 9.25 at 400 ft **SAA fired No. of rounds:** 600 **Targets:** Searchlights at Boulay and hutments, hangars and Buildings on aerodrome **DETAILS OF ATTACK:** Approached target from NW and dropped 4/112 in run from NW to SE Direct hits claimed on 2

Date /1918	Aircrew Observer G/L = gunlayer	Target	Time Out/ Time Rtn	HP O/400 Aircraft #	Details from 215 Squadron Mission Reports
					hangars in line running WSW to ENE Remainder dropped on aerodrome All bursts observed Good shooting made Visibility over target fair Searchlights not in evidence until bombs were dropped Machine glided down from 5000' to 400' and AA were unable in consequence to locate it Observations: Signalling onions in vicinity of Craincourt 8.50 to 9.50 in groups of 2s at five minute intervals 5 small fires observed in the vicinity of Courcelles 9.45 1 train stationary in station Boulay 9.20 1 train proceeding NE from Boulay Station 9.20 1 train proceeding NE from Metz Junction 9.10 **EA activity:** Nil **AA activity:** Heavy inaccurate **Searchlights:** Active and very accurate **Flaming onions:** Nil Aerodrome at Faulquement - - -
2/3 Sept	Pilot Fowler Obs Preedy G/LChalklin + Davies	Buhl Aerodrome	7.46/9.50	D4568	Dropped 16 x112 lb and 10 x 25 lb bombs at 8.56 at 600ft. Visibility poor at 4000/5000 ft and, at low altitude was good. Approach from N. **SAA fired No. of rounds:** 500 **Targets:** Sheds Hangars, Fires on Buhl Aerodrome Searchlights **DETAILS OF ATTACK:** Came in from N dropped 8/112, 10 x 25 on N end of aerodrome and 8/112 Bend (? S end) of aerodrome. Bursts observed on sheds and hangars 2 direct hits and 3 fires started Visibility at low altitude good at 4000/5000' poor **OBSERVATIONS:** SO 1 gap 2 5000 ft at intervals of 2 mins consistently (Left of course opp. aerodrome) At Buhl. Landing "L" white lights put out on approach **EA activity:** Nil

Date /1918	Aircrew Observer G/L = gunlayer	Target	Time Out/ Time Rtn	HP O/400 Aircraft #	Details from 215 Squadron Mission Reports
					AA activity: Comparatively light and accurate **Searchlights:** Active **Flaming onions:** Very active halfway between here and Buhl
2/3 Sept	Pilot Fowler Obs Preedy G/L Chalklin + Davies	Buhl Aerodrome	11.08/1.05	D4568	Dropped 16 x 112 lbs and 10 x 25 lb bombs at 12.06 at 550 ft **SAA fired No. of rounds:** 800 **Targets:** Searchlights Hutments Hangars on aerodrome **DETAILS OF ATTACK:** Approached from E Bombs dropped in one run from E to W particularly on hangars in S bend One direct hit claimed 10 coopers (25 lb bombs) in vicinity of shed on E side aerodrome Good shooting **OBSERVATIONS:** Train proceeding to Saarburg 11.50 pm **EA activity:** Nil **AA activity:** Heavy at Saarburg M.G at Buhl very active **Searchlights:** Active and accurate **Flaming onions:** Intense darkness—dropped two Michelin flares at 15 min intervals Visibility poor at 4000/5000 ft and, at low altitude was good. Approach from E. Dense darkness at the aerodrome necessitated descent to low altitude and circle the aerodrome for 15 mins
3/4 Sept	Pilot Fowler Obs Preedy G/L Chalklin + Davies	Morhange Aerodrome	7.40/9.40	D4568	Visibility very poor on way out – over target was fair. Approach from NW. Dropped 16 x 112 lb and 10 x 25 lb bombs 500 ft gliding down to 300 ft **SAA fired No. of rounds:** 700 **Targets:** Searchlights Hutments Hangars on Aerodrome **DETAILS OF ATTACK:** Approached target from NW and took one run over targets from NW to SE dropping 8/112 in two salvos of 4s gliding down to 500

Date /1918	Aircrew Observer G/L = gunlayer	Target	Time Out/ Time Rtn	HP O/400 Aircraft #	Details from 215 Squadron Mission Reports
					ft. 8/112 and 10/25 dropped at end of run at height of 300 ft. Bursts observed and machine considerably shaken. 4 direct hits claimed much damage done to hangars and aerodrome. **OBSERVATIONS:** Visibility outward very poor, visibility over target fair. Observations rendered impossible because of poor outward visibility. **EA activity:** 2 EA (type unknown) Navigation lights proceeding to land in V of Moyenville **AA activity:** Slight N of Morhange Fairly accurate **Searchlights:** Few Accurate Morhange **Flaming onions:** -
13/14 Sept	Pilot Fowler Obs Preedy G/L Fisher	Courcelles (Railway junction)	11.58/ 1.35	D4568	Dropped 16 x 112 lb and 10 x 25 lb bombs at 12.55 at 1000 ft Courcelles Station and Rail Junction **SAA fired No. of rounds:** nil **Targets:** - (left blank) **DETAILS OF ATTACK:** Approached from the W and dropped 16/112 and 10/25 in 4 salvos on objective. All bursts observed in close proximity to target and it is believed considerable damage done but proper observation was obscured by exceedingly poor visibility, thick cloud banks– and dense darkness. **OBSERVATIONS:** C not working 12.30 – 1.00 S.O. in groups of 2s in 2 min intervals 12.15 Chateau Salins S.O. 1 gap 2 S of Chateau Salins 12.15 In vicinity of Achatel – 2 white lights 200 yds apart 12.30 **EA activity:** Nil **AA activity:** Inactive and inaccurate

Date /1918	Aircrew Observer G/L = gunlayer	Target	Time Out/ Time Rtn	HP O/400 Aircraft #	Details from 215 Squadron Mission Reports
					Searchlights: Metz active **Flaming onions:** Nil
14/15 Sept	Pilot Fowler Obs Preedy G/L Fisher	Ehrang	7.52/10.15	D4568	Details of Attack: Machine ran into thick clouds in vicinity of Mohrange and it became impossible to make objective, machine being blown considerable out of course returned and landed with bombs intact
14/15 Sept	Pilot Fowler Obs Preedy G/L Fisher	Courcelles (Railway junction)	1.50/3.50	D4568	Dropped 16 x 112 lb and 10 x 25 lb bombs at 2.50 Courcelles Station and Rail Junction at 50ft followed by E to W run; again followed by strafing at 50ft Visibility poor necessitating very low flight to distinguish target. **SAA fired No. of rounds:** 400 **Targets:** Lights and searchlights in vicinity of target **DETAILS OF ATTACK:** Approached target from W and dropped 8/112 lb and 6/25 lb in first run over target from W to E Second run taken from E to W and 8/112 lb and 4/25 lb dropped. All bursts observed and 8 direct hits with 112 lb on Station and Junction **OBSERVATIONS:** All lights were extinguished on approach and visibility was poor, it being necessary to descend to very low altitude to distinguish target and effectively bomb it. Railway Station and lines were raked with MG fire. **EA activity:** - Big EA (believed Gotha) **AA activity:** 20 S of Courcelles Metz Very heavy but inaccurate **Searchlights:** 3 in v of target very accurate **Flaming onions:** General impression activity slight + N. Metz Big fire observed burning continuously between

Date /1918	Aircrew Observer G/L = gunlayer	Target	Time Out/ Time Rtn	HP O/400 Aircraft #	Details from 215 Squadron Mission Reports
					2.30 and 3.00 Boulay well lit
15/16 Sept	Pilot Fowler Obs Preedy G/L Dodd	Buhl	7.34/ 9.10	D4568	Dropped 16 x 112 lb and 10 x 25 lb bombs at 8.32 followed by strafing at 200ft **SAA fired No. of rounds:** 1200 **Targets:** Hangars and 3 machines on ground **DETAILS OF ATTACK:** Approached target from W and dropped 4/112 lb on machines all direct hits. Machines wrecked. 12/112 lb and 10/25 lb bombs on hangars in one run from W to E. Excellent shooting. All bursts observed. 10 direct hits on hangars. 3 big fires started and 2 hangars demolished Machine afterwards strafed aerodrome from 200 ft with SAA, 1200 rounds being fired at hangars and machines. Red light on aerodrome extinguished on approach. Searchlights few but inaccurate. **OBSERVATIONS:** AA barrage light and accurate. Tracer moderate and fairly accurate. Visibility exceedingly good at 200 ft and 6000 bad Train running from Saarburg S – 8.20 **EA activity:** Nil **AA activity:** **Searchlights:** **Flaming onions:**
15/16 Sept	Pilot Fowler Obs Preedy G/L Dodd	Buhl	9.53/ 11.20	D4568	Dropped 16 x 112 lb and 10 x 25 lb bombs at 10.40 170ft, followed by strafing at 100ft Conditions: Intense MG; FGO on Approach; Searchlights – some AA; Visibility good at 100 ft and bad at 3000 ft – some ground mist. **SAA fired No. of rounds:** 800 **Targets:** Hangar on Aerodrome **DETAILS OF ATTACK:** Approached target from W and dropped 16/112 + 10/25 lb bombs

Date /1918	Aircrew Observer G/L = gunlayer	Target	Time Out/ Time Rtn	HP O/400 Aircraft #	Details from 215 Squadron Mission Reports
					singly along the whole line of hangars. All bursts observed and 12 direct hits claimed. Real damage caused to hangars. Hangars were then machine gunned and 800 rounds SAA fired. Machine was riddled on all runs by tracer and ball ammunition Main petrol lead shot away and Elevators badly smashed The lateral controls were also hit and the port bottom plane is badly riddled One of the Michelin flares hit. Machine experienced difficulty in pursuing homeward course but landed safely. **OBSERVATIONS:** Saarbrücken well lit up Aerodrome and a dozen large hangars seen 1000 yd SE Buhl—with one red light in centre of aerodrome **EA activity:** Nil **AA activity:** Slight Very accurate Searchlights: Active and accurate Flaming onions: Nil M.G. very heavy
20/21 Sept	Pilot Fowler Obs Eaves G/L Ferguson	Frescaty	8.08/Not Returned	C9732	Visibility excellent and very strong westerly wind. **SAA fired No. of rounds: Targets: DETAILS OF ATTACK:** Not returned **OBSERVATIONS: EA activity: AA activity: Searchlights: Flaming onions:** FGO (S of aerodrome), AA and MG fires at Frescaty, very intense and accurate – in wide radius of the target; searchlights very accurate and active
20/21 Sept	Pilot/ Buckle Obs Preedy G/L Foulsham	Frescaty	7.43/8.25 and 9.25/9.35	D9683	14 x 112 bombs Returned owing to E.F. Made second attempt at 9.25 again returned

Date /1918	Aircrew Observer G/L = gunlayer	Target	Time Out/ Time Rtn	HP O/400 Aircraft #	Details from 215 Squadron Mission Reports
					SAA fired No. of rounds: **Targets:** **DETAILS OF ATTACK:** **OBSERVATIONS:** **EA Activity:** Nil **AA Activity:** Very heavy and accurate **Searchlights:** Very active and accurate **Flaming Onions:**
20/21 Sept	Pilot/ Kestell Obs Armitage G/L Boon	Frescaty	9.01/10.55	C9424	Dropped 14 x 112 lb bombs at 10.15 at 1000 ft **SAA fired No. of rounds:** 500 **Targets:** Hangars, sheds machines on aerodrome **DETAILS OF ATTACK:** Came in from NW but --- due to wind causing drifting to left All bursts observed and six direct hits. One hangar in NE corner observed to be hit and fire started in the proximity of 2 m/c in NE corner Visibility was perfect **OBSERVATIONS:** [Difficult to read]---heavy 9.55 to 10.20 Still bombing. S.O.between runs active ---- 9.35 to 10.35 10.50 EA seen type unknown **EA Activity:** 2 seen **AA Activity:** Around Metz, Frescaty **Searchlights:** Active **Flaming Onions:** Intense W of Metz. Active
20/21 Sept	Pilot/ Kestell Obs Armitage G/L Boon	Frescaty	11.24/2.15	C9424	Dropped 14 x 112 lb bombs at 12.50 at 1000 ft **SAA fired No. of rounds:** 1000 **Targets:** Searchlights on Target , Onion Battery to S of Target and lighted camp village N of Veruy **DETAILS OF ATTACK:** Came in from W and dropped in 4 runs S to N 14/112 lb. Machine went over target four times owing to strong wind in order to get good shooting. Hangars in SE and E. All bursts observed Six direct hits

Date /1918	Aircrew Observer G/L = gunlayer	Target	Time Out/ Time Rtn	HP O/400 Aircraft #	Details from 215 Squadron Mission Reports
					on permanent hangars and on fort to N of aerodrome. Very active Onion Batteries and AA barrage. Searchlights numerous and very active. Machine after dropping bombs descended to height of 500' severely strafing onion batteries to S of aerodrome-flowerpot Circled round for half an hour firing SAA and tracer pans Starboard prop shot through. **OBSERVATIONS:** Fire still burning at Veruy 1 ----- Metz well lit Blast furnaces very active Metz-Sablon very active and no lights extinguished while bombing Lighted camp in village N of Veruy AA Activity MG onions AA exceedingly heavy in wide radius of target Big fire in v of Saaburg 12.00/2 o'c EA 5000 (TV) over Metz 1.15 S.O. **EA Activity: AA Activity: Searchlights: Flaming Onions:**
20/21 Sept	Pilot/ Darnton Obs Murphy G/L Dallas	Frescaty	7.50/9.40	C9724	Dropped 14 x 112 lb bombs at 8.50 at 3000 ft **SAA fired No. of rounds:** 100 **Targets:** Searchlights on Frescaty Aerodrome **DETAILS OF ATTACK:** Approached from W and dropped 2/112 lb on aerodrome in proximity of hangars in one run from SW to NE. Dropped 5/112 lb on hangars. All bursts observed and 5 direct hit claimed. 7/112 lb in close proximity to sheds. Very good shooting and all bursts observed. Visibility perfect **OBSERVATIONS:**

Date /1918	Aircrew Observer G/L = gunlayer	Target	Time Out/ Time Rtn	HP O/400 Aircraft #	Details from 215 Squadron Mission Reports
					Searchlights active and accurate Frescaty Metz very well lit H.P. Machine 8.45 SW Metz 2 red lights on ground 50 yds apart halfway between Frescaty and "C" S.O. in groups of 3s Chateau Salins 8.20-9.10 S.O. in groups of 2s VY Frescaty 8.50 Fire seen at Metz Sablon 8.50 Blast furnaces NW Metz going strong **EA Activity:** Nil **AA Activity:** Inactive and inaccurate **Searchlights:** on edge of aerodrome **Flaming Onions:** Metz active
20/21 Sept	Pilot/ Darnton Obs Murphy G/L Dallas	Frescaty	11.20/12.55	C9724	Dropped 14 x 112 lb bombs at 12.10 at 1500 ft **SAA fired No. of rounds:** 350 **Targets:** Searchlights Hutments and Hangars **DETAILS OF ATTACK:** Approached aerodrome and making run from NW to SE Dropped 14/112 over field and hangars All bursts observed and direct hit claimed on large aircraft hangar AAA fire was very heavy but despite this --- good Searchlight inaccurate Flaming onions very active **OBSERVATIONS:** Train proceeding from Magnis to Metz 12— 2 red lights S.O. in groups of 2 10 miles E Frescaty 12.0- S.O. in groups of 2-3 2 mins 12.50 Chateau Salins Powerful violet searchlight in vicinity of Courcelles 12.05 Numerous lights and great activity at Metz and Metz Sablon and ---- west of Metz

59

Date /1918	Aircrew Observer G/L = gunlayer	Target	Time Out/ Time Rtn	HP O/400 Aircraft #	Details from 215 Squadron Mission Reports
					EA Activity: Nil **AA Activity:** Very heavy and accurate **Searchlights:** Very active and accurate **Flaming Onions:**
20/21	Additional Note: 4-aircraft left between 7.43 and 9.00. One aircraft returned with engine trouble (tried again at 9.25 but ET again). First: 2-aircraft reached target approaching from the W. Bombed at 1800 and 3000 ft. Bombs dropped close to the middle hangar in the line of three running E to W and in the NE corner or the aerodrome.				

*   During his squadron operational probationary time, Fowler flew five times with Captain Buck, who was well respected in 215 Squadron and who died in a landing accident when returning from a raid. Taken directly from the Squadron history: *"Capt G. S. BUCK. MC. D.F.C. Flight Commander. Born May 1897. Educated at Winchester. Was commissioned to 1st London Regt. In Nov. 1914, and served for 16 months in the front line B.E.F., Transferred to the R.F.C. in which he performed brilliant service as a Scout Pilot at Lynpo, with appointment of Flight Commander, after which he joined 215 squadron. Accomplished some splendid bombing raids notably on Armentieres, Cambrai, and Erhang Railway Jct, in which latter raid he earned the Distinguished Flying Cross. Was killed as a result of crashing upon landing after returning from a successful raid on the night of 2 September 1918."*

Figure 16: 2nd Lieutenant John Bernard (Jack) Lacy (Courtesy of his nephew, Lawrence Lacy)

Further commentary on this impressive pilot is provided from the accounts of another 215 Squadron pilot, 2nd Lieutenant John Bernard (Jack) Lacy (figure 16) who later piloted one of the four Handley Page aircraft lost in a single disastrous night 16/17 September on the raids against Cologne, Frescaty and Mannheim. Of the aircraft and crews that participated:

D9684 – 2/Lt J.B. Lacy/ 2/Lt R. Down/ Lt C.N. Yelverton

D4566 – Lt H.B. Monaghan/ Lt H.E. Hyde /2/Lt G.W. Mitchell

C9727 – 2/Lt C.C. Fisher/ 2/Lt R.S. Oakley/ Lt C.J. Locke

C9658 – Lt H.R. Dodd/ 2/Lt E.C. Jeffkins/ 2/Lt A. Fairhurst

Lacy survived a crash-landing and was taken prisoner[21] of war as were the other crews, with the exception of Dodd, who was killed in the crash landing. Lacy and the other survivors of the raid were repatriated at the end of hostilities and he died of natural causes, aged 85 in 1984. Lacy is recorded to have written of Buck, *"September 1918 started with Squadron 215 six 0/400s back to raid Ehrang rail junction and Buhl airfield. As the distance was not great, three of these returned the same night for a second attack. Opposition was intense and most aircraft arrived back damaged. One bomber, D5431, managed to land but then careered into the airfield petrol store, killing the pilot Captain G.S. Buck.... His loss in such circumstances was deeply felt by all of 215 Squadron. This "old hand" was only 21 years old when he was killed."*

Fowler, was evidently befriended by Buck, who perhaps took him 'under his wing' to show him 'the ropes' and therefore, assist him to qualify 'pilot operational.' The records show that Buck flew aggressively making low bombing attacks and this would likely have strongly impressed Fowler and was undoubtedly influential on his forming own approach achieving an average mission bombing height of only 360 feet.

---

[21] Lieutenant Hugh Monaghan (later to author his experiences under the title, "The Big Bombers of World War I"), was one of the three other pilots lost along with Lacy and he, too, was taken prisoner of war. He noted the concern that was involved with being taken into captivity, saying, "our chief worry was falling into the hands of farmers or other civilians. They hated night bombers, who they looked upon as killers of women and children and were known to pitchfork them to death. This was the fate of several German flyers downed on our side (an occurrence incidentally that is not mentioned in official records) and we expected no better." Monaghan was as lucky as was Lacy and survived the episode. An epitaph for Monaghan, written by his friend, 2/Lt Roy Shillinglaw, is included at Appendix O.

Appendix B

Notable Operational Records from the National Archives, Kew, UK

Air Wing Order No. 73, Friday 20th September, 1918:

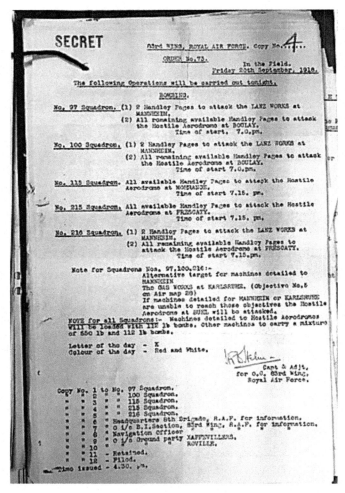

For 215 Squadron on the night 20/21 September, page text reads... *"No. 215 Squadron: All available Handley Pages to attack the Hostile Aerodrome at Frescaty. Time of start 7.15 pm."*

Intelligence Officer's 'Report on Night Bomb Raid' – Night 20/21 September, 1918:

Frescaty Aerodrome raid - casualties read: *"H.P. C9732, Pilot 2/Lt ACG Fowler, Observer 2/Lt CC Eaves Gun-layer 2/Lt JS Ferguson – Missing"*

Appendix C

Handley Page O/400 Technical Information

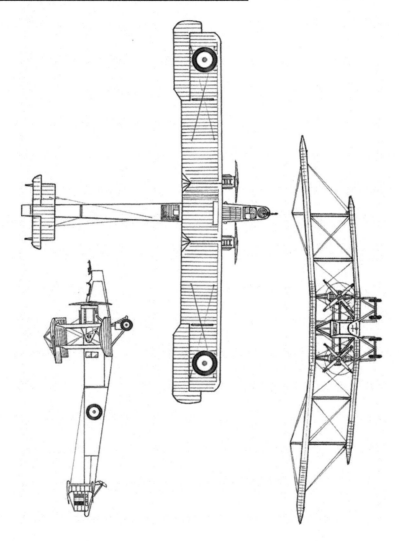

Figure 17: Handley Page O/400 Plan Views (P V Hunt CC SA 4.0)

Handley Page 0/400 C9732

General Characteristics:

Wingspan:	100 ft (30.48 m)
Length:	62 ft 10¼ in (19.16 m)
Height:	22 ft (6.71 m)
Wing area:	1,669 ft² (155 m²) (Upper wing: 1030 ft² (96 m²)
Lower wing	639 ft² (59 m²))
Weight empty:	8,502 lb (3,856 kg)
Max. Op weight:	14,022 lb (6360 kg)
Fuel Tanks:	Petrol: two in wings, two in fuselage with total capacity 200 imperial gallons/2,100 lb

Performance

Max speed:	97 mph (5,000 ft: 91.5 mph; 10,000 ft: 80 mph)
Range:	700 mi (1,120 km)
Ceiling:	10,000 ft (3,050m) (time to reach ceiling (heavy) 45 minutes)
Rate of climb:	120 ft/min (37 m/min) (23 min to climb to 5,000 ft (1,524 m))
Endurance:	8 hours
Engines:	2 Rolls-Royce Eagle VIII 360 HP (268 kW)

Armament

Guns:	4/5 x Lewis machine guns – 17 double drums (guns and mountings 200 lbs)
Bomb load:	2,000 lb (907 kg) of bombs (16 x 112 lb or 8 x 230 lb or 3 x 520 lb or 3 x 550 lb or single 1,650 lb carried on individual bomb racks or hooks – additional HE 25 lb Cooper bombs)

Handley Page O/400 Cutaway Drawing Key:

1 Twin 0.303-in (7,62-mm) Lewis guns
2 Rotatable Scarff ring
3 Gunner's cockpit (plywood construction)
4 Folding seat
5 Slat flooring
6 Entry hatch to gunner's cockpit
7 ASI pitot tube
8 Negative lens
9 Rudder pedals
10 Control wheel
11 Clear Pyralin windshield
12 Padded cockpit coaming
13 Pilot's seat
14 Observer's seat
15 Slat flooring
16 Light-bomb rack (manual)

44 Inner aileron control horn
45 Solid end ribs
46 Wing dihedral break-line
47 Gravity-feed fuel tanks in leading edge, two of 12-Imp gal (54.5-l) capacity
48 Centre-section streamlined forward cabane strut
49 Centre-section streamlined aft cabane strut
50 Forward cylindrical fuel tank (held by web straps), capacity 130 Imp gal (591 l)
51 Filler cap
52 Cross member
53 Engine control pulley cluster
54 Centre-section main bomb-bay
55 Six volt wind-driven generator (port and starboard)

70 Fuselage frame
71 Multi-strand cable bracing
72 Elevator control cable
73 Interplane streamlined spruce strut
74 Starboard rudder
75 Fabric-covered upper tailplane
76 Elevator control horn
77 Fixed surface centre-section
78 Fabric-covered elevator
79 Port rudder spruce frame
80 Port lower elevator frame
81 Fabric-covered lower tailplane
82 Rudder hinge spar
83 Plywood tail covering
84 Rear navigation light
85 Interplane strut
86 Vertical stabilizer
87 Steel attachment point
88 Faired struts
89 Tailskid
90 Removable fabric panel
91 Lifting points (stations 10 and 12)
92 Port steel cabane
93 Rear upper mainplane spar
94 Forward upper mainplane spar
95 Plywood covering
96 Steel fitting

17 Batteries
18 Trap-type forward entry door
19 Fabric lacing
20 Transparent panel
21 Plywood turtle-deck
22 Aluminium faising
23 Steel propeller hub
24 Brass tip sheathing
25 Four-blade walnut propeller
26 Radiator filler cap
27 Radiator
28 360 hp Rolls-Royce Eagle VIII engine
29 Exhaust manifold
30 Nacelle bracing strut/control spar
31 Oil tank, 15 Imp gal (68 l) in each nacelle
32 Rigging lines
33 Streamlined steel struts
34 Double flying cable braces
35 Spruce/plywood inner strut
36 Double flying cable braces
37 Single landing cable brace
38 Single stagger cables
39 Spruce/plywood outer strut
40 Double flying braces
41 Outer aileron control horn
42 Cabane braces (four point)
43 Steel cabane

56 Perforated baffle plate
57 Air-driven fuel pumps
58 Aft fuel tank, capacity 130 Imp gal (591 l)
59 Solid rib at dihedral break-line
60 Upper gunner's seat
61 Transparent panels
62 Ammunition racks
63 Ventral gunner's hatch
64 Clear Pyralin panels
65 Gunner's slatted flooring
66 Plywood bulkheads
67 Single dorsal 0.303-in (12,7-mm) Lewis gun
68 Fabric lacing
69 Control cable pulleys

Power Plant: Two 350 hp Rolls-Royce Eagle VIII 12-cylinder Vee water cooled engines driving four-blade wooden propellers of 11 ft (3.35 m) diameter.
Performance: Max speed, 97.5 mph (157 km/h) at sea level, 84.5 mph (136 km/h) at 6,500 ft (1,980 m) and 80 mph (129 km/h) at 10,000 ft (3,048 m); time to climb to 6,500 ft (1,980 m) 27 mins 10 sec; service ceiling, 8,500 ft (2,590 m).
Weights: Empty, 8,502 lb (3,857 kg); typical military load, 1,974 lb (895 kg); crew, 540 lb (245 kg); fuel and oil, 2,344 lb (1,063 kg); typical loaded weight, 13,360 lb (6,060 kg).
Dimensions: Span, upper wing, 100 ft (30.48 m), lower wing, 70 ft (21.34 m); length, 62 ft 10½ in (19.16 m); height, 22 ft (6.70 m);

dihedral, 4 deg on outer planes; track of each main undercarriage unit, 4 ft 6 in (1.37 m).
Accommodation: Normal crew of three to five, including two pilots or a pilot and observer side-by-side and front and dorsal gunners.
Armament: One or two (double-yoked) Lewis 0.303-in (7.62-mm) machine guns on Scarff ring in nose cockpit; one or two independently-mounted Lewis guns in rear cockpit and one Lewis gun firing down and aft through rear trapdoor. Internal bomb-bay to accommodate up to 16 112-lb (50.8-kg), eight 250-lb (113-kg), three 520-lb (236-kg), three 550-lb (250-kg) or one 1,650 lb (748-kg) bombs. Racks for two more bombs externally under fuselage.

97 Solid drag strut	107 Steel tube engine nacelle support struts
98 Wing structure	
99 Port aileron structure	108 Wing/fuselage attachment points
100 Port outer interplane struts (plywood-covered spruce)	109 Wing root walkway
101 Lower mainplane and rib	110 Fire extinguisher
102 Wing structure	111 Starboard undercarriage
103 Leading-edge rib construction	112 Undercarriage forward strut
104 Port inner interplane struts (plywood-covered spruce)	113 Port twin main-wheels
105 Hinge strut	114 Faired rubber chord shock strut
106 Lower mainplane dihedral break-line	115 Aft strut

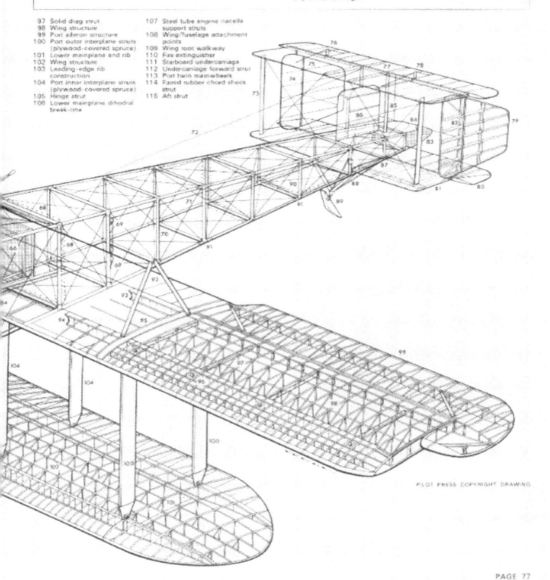

PILOT PRESS COPYRIGHT DRAWING

Figure 18: Handley Page O/400 Section – Courtesy Key Publishing Ltd., with especial thanks to Mark Ayton

Appendix D

Handley Page Armaments Referenced in the 'Short History'

Air Guns:

Figure 19: Scarff gun-ring mounting with 0.303 in (7.7 mm) twin Lewis Machine Guns and Separate Drum Magazine (U.S. Gov. Public Domain)

Air Ordnance:

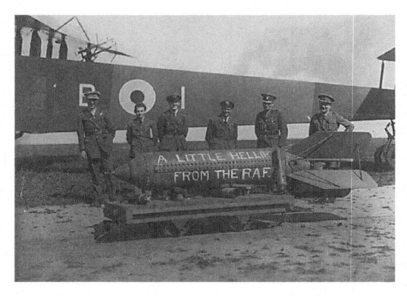

Figure 20: Officers of No. 207 Squadron RAF with a 1,650 lb HE bomb at Ligescourt near Abbeville, 29 August, 1918 (© IWM Q9971)

The 215 Squadron Bombs:

25 lb Cooper Mk 1 - Amatol filled, one detonator. Comprised a steel-cased fragmentation bomb for use against transport, aerodromes and personnel. Handley Page O/400 Gunlayers might carry 4-6 Coopers for throwing or 4 in racks.

25 lb Cooper Mk I bomb
© IWM (MUN 3258)

112 lb RL Mk I - TNT or amatol with fulminate of mercury detonator and tetryl exploder. Cast steel casing with four wind vanes. Bomb penetration enabled with a tail fuse cartridge delaying detonation from 0.25 to 15 seconds.

RL 112lb HE bomb
© IWM (MUN 3256)

SN 1,650 lb - Amatol filled but some may also have been filled with TNT. The explosive charge at 709 lb, weight would have been heavier by some 20% than any contemporary bombs. Thin cased, with nose and tail pistol fusing, it detonated immediately on impact producing high blast effects. It was designed with German industrial targets in mind, such as Essen. On the night 24/25 July, 1918, 214 Squadron C9643 dropped the first 1,650-lb. bomb in an attack on Middelkerque and although the bomb fell into a field about half a mile east of the town, the crater caused by the bomb had a diameter of over 50 feet and the spread of earth displaced covered an area over 100 yards in diameter.

1,650-lb HE bomb
OGL – v3.0

Figure 21: Handley Page O/400
Ordnance

69

Figure 22: Armourers of No. 214 Squadron RAF fusing bombs (© IWM Q11536).

Armorers of No. 214 Squadron R.A.F. fusing 112 lb and 230 lb HE bombs likely in early June 1918. Originally formed at Coudekerque, near Dunkirk, on 28th July, 1917, as No. 7A Squadron, R.N.A.S., at the outset its role was heavy night bombing. On 9th December, 1917, it became No. 14 Squadron R.N.A.S., and on 1st April, 1918 it stood up as No. 214 Squadron Royal Air Force. Not part of the Independent Air Force, under Naval Command, from 4th June to the Armistice in the 82nd Wing, it was co-opted for operations such as the Naval blockading operations at Zeebrugge and Ostend (© IWM (Q11536))

Figure 23: 10 x 112 Bomb load beneath Handley Page O/400 – From an Album (AL-25) belonging to James Faye, who served in the First World War - Repository: San Diego Air and Space Museum Archive –copyright expired

Figure 24: Armourers loading 230 lb HE bomb to an F.E. 2b, already 8x 20 lb bombs mounted to wing racks – 112 lb HE bombs lie on the ground around the front of the aircraft – alternative load 3 x 112 lb HE bombs (© IWM Q 12091)

Appendix E

World War 1 RNAS/RFC/RAF Flying Clothing and Equipment (1918)

High thigh-length, fleece-lined brown suede boots (lower left) with outer adjustable straps to the tops and with buckles and other strap and buckles to the foot and to the lower calves. They have buff leather toe caps and heels and rubber soles.

Aviator's Gauntlets with Mitten Covers):
© IWM (EQU 3844)

Aviator's RFC 'Fug' Boots:
© IWM (EQU 4040)

Coat on display at the FAA Museum, Yeovilton, UK.

Figure 25: Flight Clothing (RH Image C G Hunt CC SA 4.0)

A variety of flying gloves/gauntlets were used by RNAS/RFC/RAF aircrew. The examples on the mannequin are brown leather palmed and inside

Equipment on display at the FAA Museum, Yeovilton, UK.

Figure 26: Flight Clothing – Helmet Wear (C G Hunt CC SA 4.0)

gauntlet panel with fur covered rears. Other types included all-leather fur-lined two-in-one gloves (upper left, figure 25) with the inner being an ordinary fingered glove and the outer, a cuffed section, in the form of a fleece-lined mitten without divided fingers and without any palm.

Knee-length brown leather coat (right, figure 25) provided some protection – not fitted with a collar, because a wet fur-lined collar might freeze making for discomfort. Large fur-backed gauntlets shown are worn by the mannequin.

An open cockpit with exposure to the elements made warm clothing essential. For every 1,000 feet altitude, temperature nominally drops by 2^0 C. Aircrew wore brown leather helmets (figure 26) with ear-flaps to protect themselves from the cold temperatures, slipstream effects, rain and engine noise (two examples – one with and the other without fur surround as most suitable for sealing the type of goggles worn – see figure 26). Goggles - sometimes motor-car driving or motorcycle goggles, sometimes purchased privately - were other essential equipment.

Appendix F

215 Squadron and History

Background:
Squadron formed in France on 1 April, 1918 by renumbering No. 15(N) Squadron Royal Naval Air Service (R.N.A.S.). No. 15(N) Squadron R.N.A.S. formed previously at Couderkerque, France, on 10 March, 1918 from elements of 7(N) and 14(N) and operated the Handley Page 0/100 as a night bomber squadron against targets in Germany. After formation as 215 Squadron, Royal Air Force, it returned to England and re-equipped with the improved Handley Page O/400 before returning to France as part of the Independent Air Force as a strategic night bomber unit. The squadron disbanded on 18 October, 1919 following the end of WW I hostilities.

Basing:

Couderkerque, France	10 March, 2018
Netheravon	23 April, 1918
Andover	13 May, 1918
Alquines, France	4 July, 1918
Xaffévillers, France	19 August, 1918
Alquines, France	21 November, 1918
Ford Junction	2 February, 1919

Motto:

Surgite nox adest (Latin translation: "Arise, night is at hand"). Squadron crest (1935) - a porcupine threatened.

From History of 215 Squadron in PRO Air 1/184/15/218/1 accessed at the National Archives, Kew, UK

(*Note: Following text retains original capitalization, grammar and spelling*)

The file-folder headed:

HISTORY OF NO 215 SQUADRON ROYAL AIR FORCE
(LATE OF NO 15 SQUADRON ROYAL NAVAL AIR SERVICE)

NO. 215 HANDLEY PAGE NIGHT BOMBING SQUADRONS
ROYAL AIR FORCE.

****

HISTORICAL DATA.

****

(a). No. 215 Squadron was formed on March 10th 1918 at COUDERKERQUE AERODROME, NR. DUNKERQUE, FRANCE, and at that time, before the fusion of the R.F.C. and the R.N.A.S. was known as No. 15 Squadron, No. 5 Wing R.N.A.S.

Its Personnel – both Officers and O.R.'s – was drawn from Nos. 7 & 14 Squadrons (No. 5 Wing R.N.A.S.) respectively, Squadrons which had been operating for some time under the Command of Wing Captain C.L. Lambe R.N. (now Wing Brig. Gen. C.L. Lambe).

On April 23rd 1918 the Squadron proceeded to Netheravon, Wiltshire (No. 4 Wing R.A.F.) in order that its strength might be brought up to the requisite establishment, and subsequently move to Andover, Hants (No. 36 Wing, R.A.F.) to complete its mobilization.

(b). The Squadron proceeded Overseas on July 4th 1918 to ALQUINES AERODROME, FRANCE, under the 54th Wing, R.A.F.

(c). On August 19th 1918 the Squadron joined the INDEPENDENT FORCE (83rd Wing) at XAFFÉVILLERS AERODROME, Near NANCY, FRANCE, and subsequently returned on November 17th 1918 to ALQUINES.

(d).   It was equipped with 10 HANDLEY PAGE MACHINES fitted with EAGLE VIII. Rolls Royce Engines.

(e).   Its first and only Commanding Officer was Captain (Tempy. Major) John Fleming Jones DSC. R.A.F. who took command from the date of its inception – March 10th 1918 –

(f).   The Squadron has served in No. 5 Wing, 7th Brigade, R.N.A.S., No. 4 Wing, R.A.F., No. 36 Wing, R.A.F., No. 54 Wing, 9th Brigade, R.A.F., and No. 83rd Wing, 8th Brigade, R.A.F.

(g).   THE TOTAL WEIGHT OF BOMBS DROPPED by the Squadron is 167 tons.

(h).   Its duties have consisted entirely of NIGHT BOMBING OPERATIONS.

(i).   On the night of 11/12th April 1918, two machines of the Squadron participated with the Naval forces in the first attempt to block the entrance to OSTENDE AND ZEEBRUGGE; in spite of bad weather and wretched visibility, one H.P. Br. – Pilot Capt. J. Roy Allan DSC., and Observer Capt. Paul Bewsher DSC., attacked ZEEBRUGGE MOLE by desultory bombing for over two hours, after which proceeding to sea the machine was forced to descend owing to engine failure, the machine sank and the Pilot was drowned, but the Observer and Gunlayer were picked up in a semi-conscious condition by a British vessel. Much determination and pluck was shown by Captains Allan and Bewsher in the face of very adverse weather conditions, heavy A.A. Barrage, and intense Searchlights.

Among other notable achievements are the following:-

2.   On the night of 24/25th July 1918 eight machines attacked ARMENTIERES, dropping 7 tons of Bombs on ARMENTIERS STATION, claiming many direct hits, and fired 6350 rounds S.A.A. at ground targets. On this occasion 2/Lieut. F.E. King, though wounded, continued firing his gun until he was overcome by loss of blood; he was then removed to the lower Cock-pit, and from there took observations of the bursts of the bombs, reporting same to the Pilot.

3.   On the night of July 31st/Aug. 1st 1918 seven machines attacked FIVES RAILWAY STATION, dropping 8 tons of Bombs and firing 7750 rounds S.A.A. at ground targets.

4.   During the period of Aug. 9th to Aug. 16th 1918 (8 nights) 54 tons of bombs were dropped on CAMBRAI GARE ANNEXE, and 60,800 rounds S.A.A. were fired at various ground targets. On two consecutive nights two trips were made to objective. Great damage was achieved by this successful bombing.

5.   From July 21st to Aug. 16th 1918 nearly 89 tons of bombs were dropped on various targets.

6.   On August 19th 1918 the Squadron moved to XAFFÉVILLERS to the INDEPENDENT FORCE, and two nights after, were ready to continue operations, achieving a very successful raid on FOLPERSWEILER AERODROME, dropping over 6 tons of bombs from altitudes varying from 400' to 3000' and causing enormous damage.

7.   On the night of 23rd/24th August 1918 one machine attacked EHRANG RAILWAY JUNCTION from a height of 1500' achieving 13 direct hits. The machine was continuously in a thunder storm on its return journey for ¾ hour, becoming at times almost uncontrollable owing to the lightning. The trip was accomplished despite great difficulty, and the pilot – Capt. G.S. Buck M.C., and Observer – 2/Lieut. A.H. Barter – each received the D.F.C. in recognition of the feat.

8.   On the night of 25th/26th August two machines – Pilot Capt. W.S. Lawson, Observer Lieut. S.E. Towill; and Pilot Lieut. M.C. Purvis, Observer Lieut. W.E. Crombie, attacked the BADISCHE CHEMICAL WORKS, MANNHEIM, BUT ALTHOUGH an intense Anti-Aircraft barrage rendered approach to the target exceedingly difficult, also the Searchlights, which were extremely active and continuously blinded the Pilots, bombs were dropped from an altitude of 200', every bomb making a direct hit. These machines afterwards remained over the town and swept it with heavy S.A.A. fire, and great material damage was affected by this daring raid. On the return journey both machines passed through rain and encountered thick clouds, whilst lightning and thunder were prevalent through the trip.

On the same night four machines attacked BOULAY AERODROME, dropping three tons of bombs from a low altitude.

9.   On the night of 2/3rd September 1918 four machines attacked BUHL AERODROME and dropped 6 tons in two raids upon the Target from altitudes from 150' to 900'. These raids were accomplished in spite of exceedingly bad visibility & very heavy A.A. fire barrage, the damage in this

case was very great, three Hangars being entirely demolished and direct hits being obtained on two Motor Lorries. One machine – though very badly riddled – was brought back with consummate skill and landed without mishap; on this occasion Capt. A. Watts Williams was awarded the DFC.

10.   On the night of 14/15th September 1918 EHRANG RAILWAY JUNCTION, KAISERLAUTERN AND COURCELLES RAILWAY JUNCTIONS were attacked. One machine made three separate raids during this night, bombs were dropped at heights varying from 200' to 2000' and excellent results were obtained. The Auxiliary Petrol Tank on one machine was pierced and the back Gunlayer – 2/Lieut. S.G. Jary – climbed out and clinging to the struts stopped the leaks with his gloves, maintaining this position for ¾ of an hour; the observations in this, as on previous raids, were very valuable.

11.   On the following night – 15/16th September 1918 BUHL AERODROME AND KARLSRUHE STATION AND DOCKS were again attacked with success, two raids being again achieved; the machines were badly damaged by heavy A.A. Barrage, but were safely landed.

12.   On the night of 20/21st September 1918 two raids were again achieved, FRESCATY AERODROME being the Target, bombs were again dropped at very low altitude and much damage accomplished.

13.   On the night of 3/4th October 1918 one machine, with Capt. R.E. Darnton pilot, attacked FRESCATY AERODROME, in spite of exceedingly bad weather, four other machines having returned from this cause, and dropped all bombs from a low height, causing a large fire, direct hits were also obtained on a large bomb Dump, which exploded with tremendous force, splendid navigating, ability and skill was shown on this occasion.

14.   On the night of 23/24th October 1918 one machine – Lieut. J Lorimer – Pilot, attacked KAISERLAUTERN RAILWAY STATION, and dropped one 1600 lb. Bomb and two 112 lb. Bombs, causing considerable damage. This raid was accomplished in spite of very adverse weather conditions

15.   On the night of 10/11th November 1918 MORHANGE AND FRESCATY AERODROMES were attacked with marked success in spite of poor visibility, 10 direct hits being obtained on the Hangars.

(j).   WELL KNOWN WAR PILOTS

1.   Major J.F. Jones DSC. Squadron Commander, son of Vice Admiral J.P. Jones R.N. Born 10th April 1892. Educated at Wellington

College, Berks. Joined Canadian Expeditionary Force September 1914. Granted Commission as a Pilot in the R.N.A.S. in Sept. 1915. Flew first Handley Page machine over to France. Rose rapidly from Sub-Lieut. R.N. to Flight Commander, and was given command of a Squadron in February 1918. Was one of the Chief Pilots in the Naval Wing who were actively engaged in the bombing of Bruges, Ostende and Hun Aerodromes in Flanders, including St. Denis Westrem, the Home of the Gothas. Carried out over 40 raids in spite of excellent defence by terrific A.A. Barrage and Searchlights of these places, receiving the Distinguished Service Cross for services rendered. Belonged to the class of the "Pioneers of heavy long distance night bombing" which gave the keynote to and culminated in the splendid work of the Independent Force.

2. Capt. G.S. BUCK, MC, D.F.C. Flight Commander. Born May 1897. Educated at Winchester. Was commissioned to 1st London Regt. In Nov. 1914, and served for 16 months in the front line B.E.F. Transferred to the R.F.C. in which he performed brilliant service as a Scout Pilot, being awarded the Military Cross. Acted as Test Pilot at Lympe, with appointment of Flight Commander, after which he joined 215 Squadron. Accomplished some splendid bombing raids notably on Armentieres, Cambrai, and Ehrang Railway Jct., in which latter raid he earned the Distinguished Flying Cross. Was killed as a result of crashing upon landing after returning from a successful raid on the night of 2/3rd Sept. 1918.

3. CAPT. W.B. LAWSON. Flight Commander. Born 11th Nov. 1891. Graduated Royal Military College, Kingston, Canada. Was commissioned in the Canadian Expeditionary Forces and afterwards transferred to the R.N.A.S., proceeding East he performed very good work in bombing operations with the Indian Expeditionary Force "D" for a period of 12 months, but was invalided home suffering from Dysentry. He then became an instructor at the Eastchurch Gunnery School until he joined this Squadron in May 1918. Has achieved many successful bombing raids during the period May/Oct. 1918, and was one of the two Pilots who bombed the BADISCHE CHEMICAL WORKS, MANNHEIM, from an altitude of 200', remaining over the target for over 30 minutes. He was subsequently appointed Squadron Commander in the Canadian Flying Corps Oct. 1918.

4. CAPT. R.E. DARNTON DFC. Born 15th July 1895. Educated at Trinity College, Cambridge. Was commissioned in the R.N.V.R. in May 1915 and served with the Armoured Cars. Received his commission in the R.N.A.S. 17th Sept. 1915 and served with the Naval Wing, Dunkerque, for some time. Joined this Squadron March 1918, and has achieved many brilliant bombing raids, notable on FIVES, ARMENTIERES, CAMBRAI RAILWAY JUNCTIONS, and various enemy Aerodromes; possessing great skill as a Pilot he bombed from very low altitudes on all these occasions. The DFC. was conferred on him in January 1919 for services rendered. He was appointed Flight Commander in October 1918.

5. CAPT. A. WATTS-WILLIAMS DFC. Born May 1895. Educated at Rugby. Served as Dispatch Rider, France, 1914/1915. Was commissioned in the R.N.A.S. 20th April 1916, and served with No. 2 Wing R.N.A.S., performing some very good work. He joined 215 Squadron May 1918 and carried out many successful bombing raids, showing much Skill and daring. Was appointed Flight Commander in Oct. 1918. The DFC. was bestowed upon him as a result of zealous service.

6. CAPT. J.F. ROCHE. Born in 1887. Was commissioned in the R.N.A.S. April 1915. He joined this Squadron June, 1918, and carried out many successful bombing raids over the Lines, his bombing being greatly distinguished accuracy. He did in all over 1000 hrs. flying.

7. LIEUT. J. LORIMER. Born Feb. 1896. Was commissioned in the 19th Can. Res. Btn. C.E.F. Being seconded for duty with the Canadian R.F.C. Joined this Squadron June 1918 and accomplished excellent work in night bombing operations, on many occasions showing great skill and determination in attacking his objectives.

8. LIEUT. M.C. PURVIS. Born Feb. 1895 and was commissioned in the R.N.A.S. 28/7/17. Joined this Squadron April 1918 and acted as Gunlayer on a H.P. machine in connection with the attempt to block the entrance to Ostende and Zeebrugge, when owing to exceedingly bad weather the machine descended into the sea, and he was picked up unconscious by a British vessel. He afterwards performed very excellent work in night bombing operations, and was one of the two Pilots who bombed BADISCHE CHEMICAL WORKS from an altitude of 200'.

9. 2/LIEUT. A.C.G. FOWLER. Born June 1889 (should be 1899). Was commissioned in the R.N.A.S. 28th Oct. 1917. Joined the Squadron July 1918 and was responsible for many excellent low bombing raids; his average height from which he bombed upon eight consecutive occasions was 360'. While carrying out a raid on FRESCATY AERODROME he was shot down; buried at METZ GARRISON CEMETARY.

(k). HONOURS RECEIVED BY OFFICERS IN THE SQUADRON.

Major J.F. Jones MC	awarded D.F.C.	30.8.18
Capt. A. Watts-Williams	" "	5.9.18
Capt. R.E. Darnton	" "	Jan. 1919
2/Lieut. A.H. Watters	" "	30.8.18
2/Liut. A.K. Barter	" "	5.9.18

HONOURS RECEIVED BY N.C.O. OBSERVERS.

Sergt. E.W. Wadey	awarded D.F.M.	Oct. 1918
Sergt. W.P. Murphy	" "	Nov. 1918

Flt. Sergt. J.B. Abott	awarded M.S.M.	Jan. 1919
" C.G. Coughtrey	mentioned in Despatches	Jan. 1919

Appendix G

Handley Page O/400 Cockpit Instrumentation/Controls

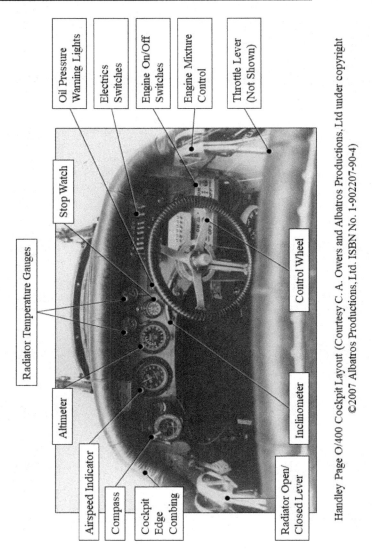

Figure 27: Handley Page O/400 Cockpit

84

Appendix H

Three Notable Missions Piloted by 2/Lt A.C.G. Fowler

1. 2/Lt Fowler evidently took to heart the admonitions of his squadron Commanding Officer, Major J.F. Jones (see below (page 88) for the recommendation for *Mention in Despatches* that was submitted for Jones [22] on 7 October, 1918, in which he is largely credited with persuading his squadron pilots to bomb from low altitude and to fly multiple raids in any one night), that low-level bombing was essential in order to hit targets successfully. Jones was relaying the direction of Major-General Trenchard. Certainly, during his time in the squadron while still qualifying to fly as captain of his own aircraft, Buck and Lawson would have impressed him with their daring and low-level attacks. A main danger of extreme low-level bombing was that a bursting-bomb fragmentation might well damage or even remove the tail of the aircraft. He followed their example and he was noted as being "responsible for many excellent low bombing[23] raids" and the "average height from which he bombed upon eight consecutive occasions was 360". An extreme example was on 14/15 Sept – a raid on Courcelles Station and Rail Junction which he made in a 50ft altitude E to W run; he again followed up by strafing at 50ft. "Visibility poor necessitating very low flight to distinguish target" – "All lights were extinguished on approach and visibility was poor, it being necessary to descend to very low altitude to distinguish target and effectively bomb it. Railway Station and lines were raked with MG fire." By any standards this was an extraordinary attack that was made in the face of enemy ground fire. (See 1, below)

2. Lands with bomb load 14/15 September after aborting raid on Ehrang, when in the area of Morhange – this was the first raid on the evening of

---

[22] Independent Force squadron Commanding Officers were not allowed or were certainly discouraged from flying on combat operations since HQ considered their administrative workload to be too large. For squadron pilots, this failure to share the risk but, nevertheless, to send others on dangerous missions involved an obvious problem. But Jones appears to have been a respected leader having, himself, flown around forty missions in Handley Pages. 215 Squadron pilot, Lieutenant Hugh Monaghan was able to recount, "although a son of an English General, was only 26 years of age and bore no signs of a stiff-necked upbringing."

[23] Low bombing "by eye", given the inaccuracy of the Drift Sight, produced more successful results for bombs on target. 215 Squadron pilot, Lieutenant Monaghan noted this saying that it was "for this reason some of us preferred to go low and release by sight." But, while exposed to machine-gun fire when at low level, it also allowed avoidance of AA fire, "one chanced a direct hit but I always thought this was less risky than the spread of shrapnel higher up."

14 September. Landing at night in the Handley Page O/400 was tricky for a variety of reasons including time when airfield lights were extinguished because of suspected enemy air activity. Landing with a bomb hang-up might always be a cause for concern in case it shifted in the landing impact or it might fuse. Landing with a full bomb load meant that the aircraft was landing 'heavy' presenting control difficulties for the pilot. If the aircraft broke up in the landing, having high-explosive bombs loose increased the risk of an inadvertent detonation. Having taken off at 19:52 D4568 returned to Xaffévillers at 22:15 to make a landing with bombs still on board: "Machine ran into clouds in vicinity of Morhange and it became impossible to make the objective being blown considerably out of course so returned and landed with Bombs intact." 2/Lt Fowler's landing was an achievement in itself and with the aircraft refueled and serviced, Fowler and his crew of observer 2/Lt Preedy and Gunlayer Fisher took off again at 01:50 on the morning of 15 September for their second raid. (See 2, below)

3. 15/16 September 2/Lt Fowler and his crew of observer 2/Lt Preedy and Gunlayer Fisher attacked Buhl Aerodrome for a second time that night. Their earlier mission was a sortie from 19:34 to 21:10 and they had dropped 16/112 lb and 10/25 lb bombs and strafed the aerodrome in the face of moderate but accurate ground fire. For their second mission, they took off at 21:53 and approached target from W and dropped 16/112 + 10/25 lb bombs singly along the whole line of hangars. "All bursts observed and 12 direct hits claimed. Real damage caused to hangars. Hangars were then machine gunned and 800 rounds SAA fired." His bombing runs were conducted at 170 ft, followed by strafing runs along the airfield at 100 ft. In the after-action report, Fowler notes that AA fire is slight but very accurate, searchlights accurate and active and machine-gun fire is very heavy. D4568 was badly hit in a number of areas and recounted in the report that it was "riddled on all runs by tracer and ball ammunition. Main petrol lead shot away and Elevators badly smashed. The lateral controls were also hit and the port bottom plane is badly riddled. One of the Michelin flares hit." The damage was certainly extensive and very serious and the aircraft could only be controlled with difficulty and is described as "machine experienced difficulty in pursuing homeward course but landed safely." The damaged is estimated in figure 28, (See 3 below)

1. 14/15 September attack - D4568 drops 16 x 112 lb and 10 x 25 lb bombs at 02:50 Courcelles Station Rail Junction at 50 ft followed by E to W run; again followed by strafing at 50 ft (TNA Kew UK):

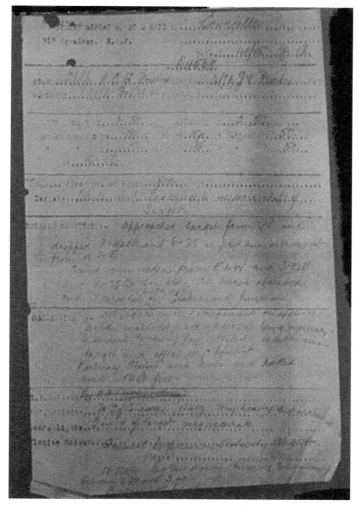

Observations: "All lights were extinguished on approach and visibility was poor, it being necessary to descend to very low altitude to distinguish target and effectively bomb it. Railway Station and lines were raked with MG fire."

Recommendation for Mention in Despatches written by the Officer
Commanding the 83rd Wing for his subordinate No. 215 Squadron
Commander, Major John Fleming Jones (TNA Kew UK).

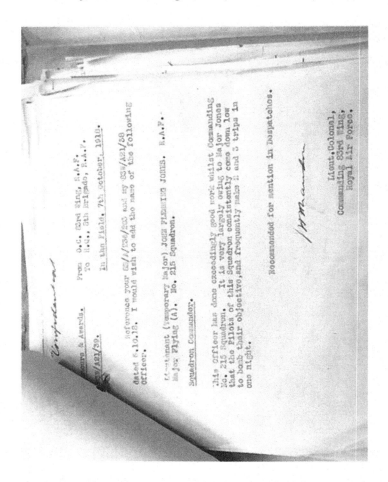

*"This officer has done exceedingly good work whilst Commanding No. 215
Squadron . It is very largely owing to Major Jones that the Pilots of this
Squadron consistently came down low to bomb their objectives, and
frequently made 2 and 3 trips in one night."*

2. 14/15 September Raid on Ehrang Rail Junction – extract on after
    action report follows (TNA Kew UK):

The after action report reads: *"Machine ran into clouds in vicinity of Morhange and it became impossible to make the objective being blown considerably out of course so returned and landed with Bombs intact"*

3.   15/16 September D4568 raid on Buhl Aerodrome

Handley Page O/400, D4568 – Showing the extent of estimated battle damage
sustained during the night 15/16 September raid on Buhl Aerodrome

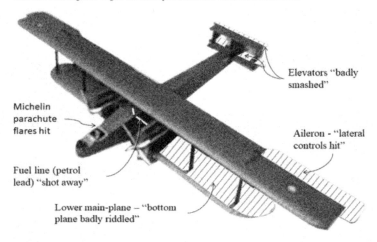

Elevators "badly
smashed"

Michelin
parachute
flares hit

Aileron - "lateral
controls hit"

Fuel line (petrol
lead) "shot away"

Lower main-plane – "bottom
plane badly riddled"

Handley Page O/400 of 214 Squadron, at Saint-Inglevert Aerodrome,
Pas-de-Calais, France. Possibly C9674 damaged 21/22 August in an
attack on Bruges docks and a followed by a sustained attack by an
enemy fighter. Note scale of the damage to the lower starboard wing.
The aircraft was returned to missions by 15 September 1918
(Copyright expired, before 1 January 1923)

Figure 28: Likely damage to D4568 (upper image: P V Hunt CC SA 4.0) and
actual damage to C9674 showing how surface canvas covering is torn away
after sustaining gunfire and slipstream tear damage

Appendix I

Locations of 2/Lt A.C.G. Fowler's Mission Targets

Marks Raid Target (Map - Wikimedia Commons US Govt Public Domain)

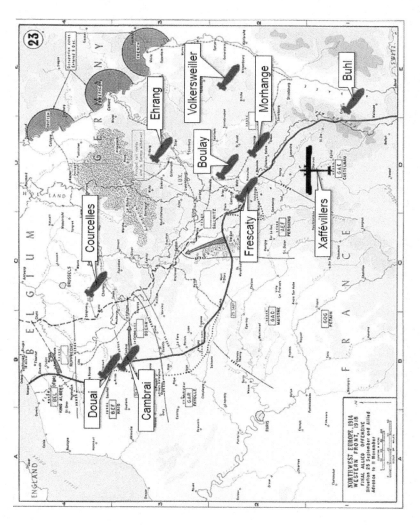

Figure 29: Targets attacked by 2/Lt. Fowler 6/7 August to 20/21 September, 1918.

Appendix J

Details of 2/LT A.C.G. Fowler's targets, crew role and the estimated time of attack during the period of his operational service, August-September 1918

No.	Date /1918	Target	Crew Status	Time Over Target
1	6/7 August	Railway annexe betw Blance Maison /Douai	Passenger	11.30 pm
2	9/10 August	Cambrai Rail Junction Mission aborted with engine failure	Passenger	-
3	10/11 August	Cambrai Gare Annexe	Gunlayer	10.40 pm
4	11/12 August	Cambrai (SE) Railway Annexe	Gunlayer	10.56 pm
5	12/13 August	Unknown	Gunlayer	10.50 pm
6	13/14 August	Cambrai Gare Annexe	Gunlayer	10.47 pm
7	14/15 August	Cambrai Gare Annexe	Pilot	11.20 pm
8	15/16 August	Cambrai Gare Annexe	Gunlayer	10.30 pm
9	22/23 August	Volkersweiller (Folpersweiller) Aerodrome	Pilot	11.16 pm
10	23/24 August	Boulay Aerodrome	Pilot	9.35 pm
11	25/26 August	Boulay Aerodrome	Pilot	9.26 pm
12	30/31 August	Boulay Aerodrome	Pilot	9.25 pm
13/14	2/3 September	Buhl Aerodrome	Pilot	8.56 pm / 12.06 am
15	3/4 September	Morhange Aerodrome	Pilot	~8.40 pm
16	13/14 September	Courcelles Rail Junction	Pilot	12.55 am
17/18	14/15 September	Erhang – Bad weather – Mission aborted. Courcelles Rail Junction	Pilot	10.15 pm/ 2.50 am
19/20	15/16 September	Courcelles Rail Junction	Pilot	8.32 pm/ 10.40 pm
21	20/21 September	Frescaty Aerodrome	Pilot	~9.20 pm

Appendix K

The Independent Force

The Zeppelin raids on Britain in 1915 and 1916 and the first air raid by twin-engined Gotha bomber aircraft on 25 May, 1917 followed by the first daylight raid on London, causing 162 deaths and 432 injuries on 13 June 1917 caused a public outcry and the government came under an obligation to counter the attacks quickly. The carnage in France on the Western Front was massive but it was over the channel and, therefore, somewhat removed in the national psyche and, although tens of thousands were being killed in the front lines, to many, warfare seemed remote. However, the attacks by the German raiders on London and elsewhere in Britain, despite civilian killed being only numbered in a few thousand - comparatively small versus the uniformed losses – resulted in outrage, fright and (from a Government aspect) a threat to public morale. There was an immediate demand to counter the threat and new air defences were developed. At nights, a blackout was observed and anti-aircraft guns, searchlights and observers were deployed. Fighter aircraft were brought back from France to defend the homeland. Incendiary ammunition was developed for fighters attacking the Zeppelins in order to destroy them by igniting their hydrogen lifting gas, if they could achieve an interception (the high altitude remained a problem throughout the period of active Zeppelin operations). For example, on the night of 1 October 1916, the Zeppelin L.31 was headed towards London but when caught in searchlights, the commander elected to abandon the raid and dropped his bomb load to lighten the airship and increase height (the bombs were reported to have fallen and injured a woman in Cheshunt, Hertfordshire, which lies within the London metropolitan area). Flying a B.E.2c fighter and at ~14,500 feet, at around 11:45pm, Lieutenant Wulstan J. Tempest saw the Zeppelin at about 15-miles distant. He intercepted and took fire from the defending Zeppelin crew and in his second pass, his incendiary fire ignited the airship from which flames erupted and it fell hitting the ground at Potters Bar. So exhausted by the cold and his exertions, he crashed his BE.2c on landing, slightly fracturing his skull against the butt of his machine gun!

Despite this type of fight-back, Parliament, animated by outraged public sentiment, demanded more. The Prime Minister, Lloyd George, tasked General Jan Smuts, the former Boer War guerilla and now member of the War Cabinet, to conduct a study and to make recommendations for air defence, air forces and air support. Smuts identified the value of air power as a strategic weapon that had value quite independently of support to ground or maritime operations. He reported back to cabinet that air operations possessed the potential to devastate "enemy lands and (the) destruction of industrial and populous centres on a vast scale and may become the principal operations of war, to which older forms of military and naval operations may become secondary and subordinate." Smuts understood very clearly that wars might be won behind the lines of trenches by the systematic destruction of the infrastructure that was strategically vital to the maintenance of field armies or ships. This might be by destroying the ability to produce steel, food, fuel...or the morale and the will to endure of the general population. Smuts was a 'child of his military experience' and mass bombing behind enemy lines was akin to mounted Boer guerrilla warfare on a very grand scale and with a new-age weaponry approach. He saw that military and naval interests were only indirectly linked to the prosecution of strategic targets and he recommended a combination of the Royal Flying Corps (R.F.C.) and the Royal Naval Air Service (R.N.A.S.) under a separate new organization – an Air Ministry alongside the Admiralty Board and General Staffs. The War Cabinet accepted Smuts' recommendations on 24 August, 1917.

To Field Marshal Douglas Haig, the Commander of the British Expeditionary Force (B.E.F.) in France from late 1915 until the end of the war, the amalgamation of the R.F.C., and R.N.A.S., was a dangerous anathema that would divert vital air resources and thereby weaken operations on the Western Front. Major-General Hugh M. Trenchard, Commander of the R.F.C., in France was of the same mind and was opposed to the establishment of an Air Ministry. Nevertheless, the War Cabinet pressed forward and the Air Council and Air Ministry were created on 3 January, 1918. The Air Council was established under the presidency of Lord Rothermere and, somewhat surprisingly and much to the chagrin of Haig who wanted to keep him in France, Trenchard was prevailed upon to become Chief of the Air Staff.

Personal antagonisms and professional differences between Trenchard and the Air Minister, Lord Rothermere were legion. Trenchard's tenure as the first chief of Air Staff was a mere ten-weeks from 18 January to 12 April, 1918. Rothermere resigned on 26 April, 1918, barely a fortnight after Trenchard's departure, to be succeeded by Sir William D. Weir in his role as President of the Air Council. Maj-Gen Fredrick Sykes succeeded as the new Chief of the Air Staff (CAS). A longtime rival of Trenchard, (who exemplified the 'warrior' and who inspired by example), Sykes epitomized the calculating manager and was apparently loathed by Trenchard. Weir, as the new secretary of state for the Royal Air Force, assumed his position on

27 April, 1918. He sought to bring Trenchard, who by the normal standards of behavior was somewhat petulant (and a number of contemporaries apparently thought this of him, exactly), back into the fold offering him any one of a series of posts; he was ultimately successful, convincing Trenchard to accept the position of General Officer Commanding (GOC), Independent Force, an "independent command" for long range bombing forces in France. It was left to the Air Ministry to clarify formally to the Government War Cabinet that the purpose of Trenchard's new command was "to constitute an Independent Force, Royal Air Force, for the purpose of carrying out bombing raids on Germany on a large scale." He took up command of the Independent Force, on 6 June, 1918.

Trenchard had stipulated that as commander of the Independent Force he would work directly for-and take orders solely from-Weir. So that there could be no doubt about this, he wrote in addition to his acceptance to Weir, that he took over on the explicit understanding that he would "take over administration of all R.A.F. units in Independent Force" ...and the "Independent Force will deal direct with you (Weir) on all matters." At a stroke, Sykes was bypassed and Weir, Syke's superior in the Air Ministry, ensured that Trenchard enjoyed full freedom from interference by the CAS – an extraordinary situation and an absolute anathema to the usual maxims of responsibility and accountability. However, such was the power of Trenchard's cachet of personal standing that his demand for autonomy was granted by Weir. A major problem with this was that Trenchard was cut off from a pool of air operations and staff experience that might have provided much needed good aviation judgment – let alone that unconstrained, he was able to operate like a potentate, such was the loose supervision applied by Weir. The upshot was that Sykes, somewhat cold, calculating and uncharismatic, became superfluous to the Independent Force strategic bombing initiative with Trenchard inclined, for professional and personal reasons, to ignore him.

The raison d'être of the Independent Force was that it was just that – it was established to be independent, to attack and destroy such targets that constituted the raw materials of war or production thereof. Such strategic targets include the chemical industry, fuel production, rubber production, coal mining, food-processing and so on...to include, perhaps, the morale and will to endure of a civilian population. It was not to be employed in support of direct land or sea operations (i.e. tactical employment).

Seeking to constrain Trenchard, Sykes prohibited the Independent Force from attacking such tactical targets as aerodromes and railways.

Strategic targets at long range like the German chemical industry, suppliers of raw materials for explosives, propellants, and poison gas were to be the strict focus of operations although steel works were acceptable, if poor weather intervened. Within a short period of taking over the Independent Force, Trenchard had shown how he could ignore the direction of the Air Staff by changing directives to conform to his own views of how the bombing campaign should be waged and, furthermore, he exploited the media with great effect to publicise raids on railways, aerodromes and infrastructure and, thereby, secure favorable public repute. By July 1918, a month after Trenchard's assumption of IF command, the problems between Trenchard and Sykes had spread down to their staffs as an essentially complete rift with Sykes's Independent Force policy of targeting priorities, largely ignored. Indeed, Major Tiverton, a ministry expert on target selection and related technical matters, reported that of the "systematic choice of key industries (that) was begun upon paper and the chemical targets definitely chosen for priority. In fact the I.F. have not systematically attacked them, or even attempted to do so." Furthermore, he noted that of the 245 Independent Force attacks though the period April-July 1918, only 32 had been directed against these objectives with the "vast majority (were) undertaken against railway sidings and enemy aerodromes." Trenchard, appears to have been somewhat possessed of his own importance, with maintaining his independence from the Air Ministry (Sykes in particular) and was not going to allow "any officer in London" to interfere with his choices of target selection. He was resistant to the concept of strategic bombing and primarily used the Independent Force to support military operations close to the front line. While flouting and frustrating the War Cabinet directive for an independent strategic-bombing force, Trenchard undoubtedly pleased the French and British field commanders in France, Marshal Foch and Field Marshal Haig respectively.

Trenchard created his own "Air Staff Branch, H.Q., I.F.," in Autigny-la-Tour, France, that duplicated the London-based Air Staff under Sykes. It comprised all of the components required to conduct fully independent bombing operations and thereby, it provided the self-sufficiency that Trenchard sought to preserve personal autonomy. Trenchard made some concessions to create the impression that the Independent Force was indeed conducting strategic operations and a limited number of raids on Germany were conducted as de facto evidence. If only done for appearances, since he had to report to Weir, and this involved War Cabinet oversight, these targets were not the same as the objectives that he ordered his commanders to raid. He appears to have concealed from his superior the fact that he intended to raid enemy railways and aerodromes contrary Air Ministry instruction. After the battle for the St. Mihiel Salient in September, in an interview with the Daily Mail, Trenchard appeared to concede some value to strategic bombing noting that a few bombing attacks on German civilian populations hurt morale and instigated a disproportionate enemy response to withdraw some weaponry from the front lines and redeploy it for air defence purposes – just as the old Boer, Jan Smuts, had anticipated. However, by war's end, thoroughly outrageously, Trenchard was able to refer to his Command, the Independent Force, as "a more gigantic waste of effort and personnel there has never been in any war."

Trenchard, in his writings after the end of hostilities, considered the Independent Force to be the failure that he had anticipated at outset and presumably, since characterized as a "failure", it provided the rationale and the alibi for having ignored the formal operational directives from the Air Ministry. He evidently considered himself vindicated by dint of his initial unwillingness to accept the Independent Force Command when chivvied by Weir. He was, quite clearly, the reluctant Commander and his price to serve was Weir's promise of the independence of his new Command and, especially, his freedom from any effective interference by Sykes. Between June and the end of hostilities in November 1918, the Independent Force lost 138 aircraft to enemy action and 320 aircraft to air accidents associated with combat operations. What appears to be extraordinary as the pages of history are turned back on Trenchard's actions are the character failings, the conceit, egotism and vanity; the flaunting of chain of command, deceit and peevishness when not getting his own way. To be fair to Trenchard, he was probably not alone in an age when the accoutrements of influence, rank and power may yet have outweighed professional ability, competence and accountability. However, this apparently flawed man held the lives of so many aircrews in his hands and sent them to war facing horrific odds and conducting missions that were counter to the orders that he had received. He did not believe in the Independent Force strategic bombing mission and chose to use his allocated squadrons somewhat as a private air force on targets that, apparently, he personally determined. He appears to show a rather callous disregard for the flying dangers and the need to preserve precious aircraft and aircrew when he lectured the new 216 Squadron Commanding Officer, Maj W. R. Read, saying, "Well, I have got you out here to take over 216 Squadron from Buss. They have got Naval ideas. They think they cannot fly at night if there is a cloud in the sky and they think they cannot do more than one raid in a night. You have got to get them out of those ideas."

The operational life of the Independent Force 'experiment' was really very short – Trenchard's tenure in Command during hostilities was 5 June (tactical command)/15 June 1918 (administrative and full command) through to January 1919. The original 41st Air Wing was raised to Brigade level as the VIII Brigade under the Command of Brigadier-General C.L.N.

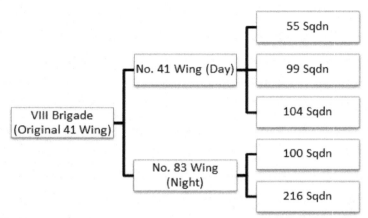

Newall[24] on 28 December 1917. Under the VIII Brigade, the component 41st Wing was reconstituted into the 41st and 83rd air wings as basis of the Independent Force. The 41st Wing (Day) comprised, 55 (DH.4) and 99 (DH.9) squadrons and the 83rd Wing (Night), 100 (FE.2b) and 216 (Handley Page O/400) squadrons. Shortly later, 104 (DH.9) joined the 41st Wing as an additional day-bombing squadron. The establishment of the Independent

---

[24] Command of Brigadier-General C.L.N Newall flew as a flight commander with No. 1 Squadron with the BEF in 1914 and in March 1915, he was given command of No. 12 Squadron operating BE2c aircraft bombing railways and conducting reconnaissance. After taking command, he took himself off combat operations intent on administrative duties, and was reportedly not well regarded by his men for this. He recovered somewhat with an act of courage in which he helped extinguish a fire in a bomb store and was recommended for an award by Major-General Trenchard. In October 1917, he took command of the newly formed 41st Wing and when upgraded to become the VIII Brigade, he was promoted to Brigadier General. When the VIII Brigade was subsumed as the basis of the Independent Force in June 1918, he handed over command to Trenchard and was himself appointed Deputy Commander of the same. Later to rise to be Chief of the Air Staff, he was forced into early retirement following the Battle Britain when he ran foul of Prime Minister Churchill over the issue of confidence in his leadership of the R.A.F.

Force by Trenchard was a significant logistic undertaking but with work already in hand by Newall to construct aerodromes, he focused on the "formation of a large staff" to assure that his Command in France could be "completely independent" of London interference. This staff was established near Nancy, France and was operational by 26 June 1918. The work on the aerodromes took longer and was not complete until just before the end of hostilities in November 1918 – the scale of the work was significant and, for example, at Xaffévillers, some 60 miles of drains were laid and the field leveled and sown with grass seed.

Royal Aircraft Factory F.E.2b about to start out upon a night raid. Taken under (© IWM (Q12229))

Trenchard had absorbed the lesson, from his time commanding the R.F.C. aircraft of the British Expeditionary Force (B.E.F.), that it was a necessity to be equipped with "*sufficient aircraft to hold and beat the German aerial forces on the Western Front*" although curiously, he does not make an equal

Royal Aircraft Factory F.E.2b seen from above (© IWM (Q 69317))

Figure 30: F.E. 2b Night Bombers

point that superior technology and performance are also vital. Strategic bombing on German territory, he believed, would be a luxury until German air forces were beaten (perhaps a lesson learned from the "Bloody April" experience in 1917[25]), however, with this completed, he favored taking the attack to what he called "the German Army in Germany", so to cripple sources of supply. He considered two approaches, the first being to attack a main urban-industrial centres singly and to devastate it before moving on to the next. The second, to attack as many large urban-industrial centers as possible, each with just a few aircraft and thereby, increase enemy uncertainty about where attacks might occur prompting a response to dilute home defences or weaken Western Front forces by withdrawing front line equipment. Having too few aircraft to do massive material damage, he chose the second option, however, his prosecution of urban-industrial centres with sporadic raids took second place to his attacks against railways and aerodromes which were certainly made with the intention not just causing damage but rather full dislocation of their ability to continue in operation. Nevertheless, whether or not the towns and centers of Germany received only a minority of the Independent Force bombing effort, certainly the aerial assault involved many widespread target locations (see map at figure 31) even though material destruction was reported to be relatively light. It will be worthwhile to return to consider Trenchard's other motivation for this dissipated attack campaign strategy later in this treatise.

In a written submission to Weir dated 1 January, 1919, Trenchard stated his belief that, "before it was possible to attack Germany successfully (author note: meaning - strategic German targets) it was necessary to attack the enemy's aerodromes heavily in order to prevent his attacking our aerodromes by night, and by destroying his machines to render his attacks by day, less efficacious. [He] considered that it was probable during the spring and early summer of 1919 that at least half [his] force would be attacking the enemy's aerodromes, whilst the other half carried out attacks on long-distance targets in Germany". He added to this that, from time to time, he had conducted attacks in support of Western-Front ground operations and that he had prioritized railways as targets, ahead of blast furnaces. Trenchard clearly favored the tactical employment of the Independent Force and, although counter to the operational mandate that he was given, and much to the frustration of Sykes, the rationale to destroy and harry enemy air forces

---

[25] Bloody April refers to spring 1917 during which British aerial support of the Battle of Arras resulted in very heavy R.F.C. casualties at the hands of the German *Luftstreitkräfte*. Trenchard, commanding the R.F.C., supported the offensive use of air power but despite committing superior numbers of combat aircraft to the air battles, his squadrons took disproportionate losses, since larger numbers proved less seminal in combat outcomes than the technical superiority and pilot training of German fighter aircraft at that time. However, the R.F.C. action contributed to the success of the 5-week Allied ground campaign.

on the ground has much to commend it, influenced, no doubt, by Bloody April.

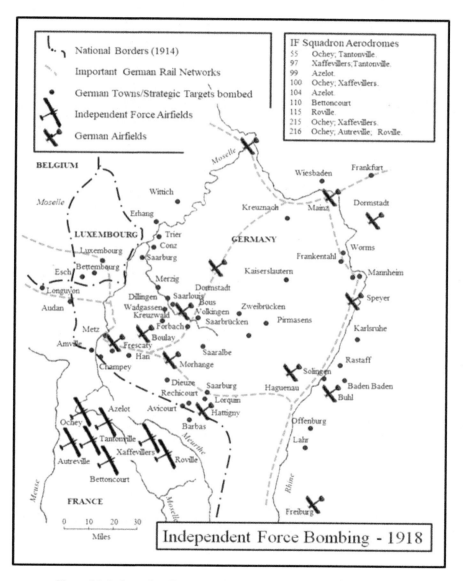

Figure 31: Independent Force Bombed Targets (P V Hunt CC SA 4.0)

His force was increased by four additional squadrons on respectively 9, 19, 31 and again, 31 August by 97 (Handley Page O/400), 215 (Handley Page O/400), 115 (Handley Page O/400), and 110 (DH.9A). Lastly, on 22 September, 45 (Sopwith Camel) was added to provide fighter interdiction capability to attack enemy scout aircraft deep behind the front

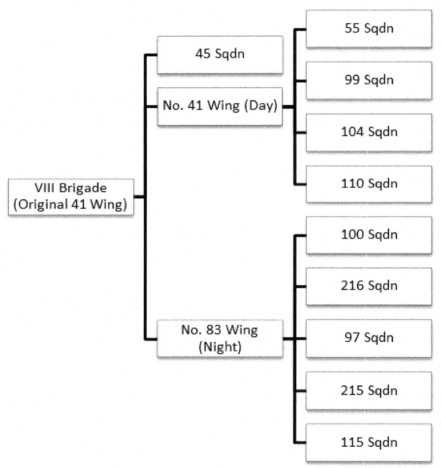

line. The Independent Force was divided into two units with the DH.4-9/9A raiding by day and the Handley Page and F.E.2b (see figure 30) by night. Although night bombing was considered safer in respect of lesser enemy anti-aircraft measures (but not for accidents due to limited visibility at night, adverse weather and difficult landings) than was day bombing, Trenchard believed that the proportion of day squadrons should exceed night squadrons. This was despite very heavy day losses which required some of his squadrons to stand-down due to the loss of war-fighting cohesion resulting from the loss of experienced aircrew and shock of battle. Despite higher casualties, day bombing was more accurate and he argued that it caused the enemy to invest more manpower and material in counter air measures.

Several types of aircraft were incorporated into the Independent Force and were representative of the fast-developing aeronautic technology of the day which was able to field a new design within months rather than the two-decades required for a twenty-first century fighter. Adaptation was also evident, whereby, for example, the shortage of manufactured engines or other materials might require performance compromise as alternative solutions were forced upon the aircraft producers. Aircraft such as the F.E. 2b, by 1917, were obsolete as fighters but might find a new role in night operations where any performance shortcomings were diminished. The aircraft fell into two categories, either day or night intruders:

The Day Bombers:

DH.4 - Predominantly, the day squadrons operated the two-seat DH.4 and later 9/9A variants. The DH.4 was two-aircrew biplane of wood and fabric construction with the forward fuselage and the underside of the tail area covered by a 3mm plywood skin. Powered by a 270 h.p. Rolls-Royce Eagle, the aircraft was armed with a single forward-firing Vickers machine gun and either one or two 0.303 in (7.7 mm) Lewis guns on a Scarff ring, fired from the observer's rear cockpit. The DH.4 had a maximum speed of 143 mph (230 km/h) at sea level, a range of 470 mi (770 km) with a maximum endurance of 3¾ hours and a service ceiling of 22,000 ft (6,700 m). The maximum bomb load was 460 lb (210 kg) carried on external under-fuselage/wing racks. The DH.4 was arguably the best single-engined bomber of World War I and was well liked by its crews. Lt Leonard Miller, who wrote an unofficial history of No. 55 Squadron, accounted "that the D.H.4 was a success" and the squadron song, "In Formation" (Appendix P refers), praised its qualities in a way that only a raucous refrain is able. With the Eagle engine installation, its performance countered some of the shortcomings that bomber aircraft usually concede to fast and agile fighter aircraft. To this extent, the DH.4 would fly raids over enemy territory without a friendly-fighter escort. The 55 squadron DH.4s of the Independent Force developed tactics of flying in close V-formations which

103

allowed concentrated defensive fire from the rear cockpits to fight off German fighter attacks.

DH.9 - There was a severe shortage of Rolls-Royce Eagle engines and so the DH.9 was designed to use an alternative engine and to introduce a number of improvements. With the DH.4, it shared many of the same airframe components (wings and tail unit) but it used a new fuselage that moved the pilot and observer cockpits closer together and away from the engine and fuel tank, which improved communication and air-fighting effectiveness. Novel internal stowage was provided to carry two 230 lb or four 112 lb bombs, however, external carriage was preferred operationally. A new engine, a Beardmore-Halford-Pullinger (BHP)/Galloway 'Adriatic,' promised to increase aircraft performance based on the development BHP engine rating of 300 h.p. which was more powerful than the Eagle. The Galloway Adriatic engine was fitted to the prototype DH.9 but unfortunately, because of production manufacturing modifications it produced only, 200 h.p. Production DH.9s were fitted with the Siddeley Puma, also based on the BHP engine and, similarly, it too only produced 200 h.p. When the DH.9 entered service, it was recognized quickly that its flying performance was inferior to the DH.4 aircraft that it was intended to replace. The DH.9's performance in combat was disastrous because of both low engine power and failures due to engine unreliability despite it being de-rated. The DH.9 proved to have a maximum speed of 113 mph (182 km/h) at sea level, a range of 470 mi (770 km) with a maximum endurance of 4½ hours and a service ceiling of 15,500 ft (4,730 m). The reduction in service ceiling from the D.H.4 22,000 ft was particularly detrimental to combat capability. During the period June-December 1918, the Independent Force 99 and 104 DH.9 squadrons were mauled with 54 aircraft lost in air combat and an additional 94 critically damaged in operating accidents and these losses were, in part, attributed to the DH.9 shortcomings. Brevet Colonel J.M. Salmond, General Officer Commanding the Royal Flying Corps in the Field in France (to become Chief of the Air Staff in 1930), explained the plight of the DH.9 very well, reporting in October, 1918, that it could only be used without unacceptably high losses if there was local air superiority. He wrote, "This is demonstrably true, at present time, of DH.9 Squadrons with 200 hp BHP engines, for although this type of aeroplane has sufficient petrol, and oil, to enable it to reach objectives 100 miles from the lines, its low ceiling, and inferior performance oblige it to accept battle when, and where, the defending (enemy) forces choose, with the practical result that raids tend to become restricted to those areas within which protection can be afforded by the daily offensive patrol of scout squadrons." Trenchard too, who well understood and had complained to Weir about the performance shortcomings of the DH.9, by the end of August 1918, recognized that the losses sustained by unescorted DH.9 did not justify sending them raiding. o

Independent Force 110 Squadron DH.9A

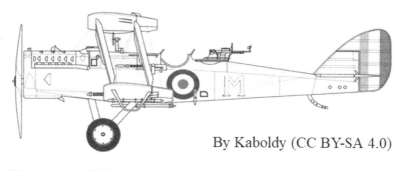

By Kaboldy (CC BY-SA 4.0)

4 x 25 lb Cooper bombs carried DH.9A under-wing racks (Courtesy RAF Museum, Hendon)

Figure 32: Independent Force No. 110 DH.9A Day Bomber

There was a demand for an improved design in response to the disappointing DH.9 performance which resulted from the underpowered and unreliable BHP-based engines. The answer was the DH.9A (figure 32) which employed a more powerful engine and, since the shortage of sufficient numbers of Rolls-Royce Eagle engines was ongoing, it used the newly available US 400 h.p. (298 kW) Packard V12 Liberty engine. DH.9As were produced by the Westland Aircraft works at Yeovil, UK and were delivered to 110 squadron[26], who deployed to Bettoncourt, France, as part of the Independent Force on 31August, 1918. Their first operational mission was a daylight raid on the German aerodrome of Boulay on 14 September, 1918. Despite the improvement in performance resulting from the Liberty engine, the DH.9A squadrons still suffered high losses during long-range interdiction missions into Germany. The maximum bomb load of the DH.9A was increased to 740 lb (336 kg) carried on underwing and fuselage racks. It proved to have a maximum speed of 123 mph (198 km/h) at sea level, a range of 470 mi (770 km) with an maximum endurance of 5 ¼ hours and a service ceiling of 16,750 ft (5,110 m) and an absolute ceiling of 18,000 ft – still slower and lower than the DH.4 but endurance and ordnance load increased. In later 1918, day bombing tactics had still not developed beyond the V-formation six-ship wedge that was common in 1917. An Independent Force day-bomber squadron of 18-aircraft might put up 12 serviceable aircraft from the pool arranged in two V-formations in a sort of "follow-the-leader" arrangement. Squadron practice was to fly to a high altitude of 17,000 feet which could be maintained with a bomb load of three 112lb bombs and to maintain a tight V-formation during ingress and egress to the target, bomb release and especially when under attack. The high altitude and close formation provided some protection against enemy fighters whose own speed and maneuver performance was degraded as a result of altitude effects and it allowed concentration of D.H.9 rear-gunner defensive fires. A measure of the mortal challenge faced by day bombers is illustrated by two notable D.H.9A raids. First, on 25 September, 1918 two formations of six 110 Squadron aircraft launched to carry out a daylight bombing raid on works and railways at Frankfurt. One DH.9A returned early as a result of mechanical problems and force landed. Take-off had been 09:55 and the railway target was bombed at 12:05 with total mission time, five and a half hours. Four D.H.9A aircraft were lost to enemy

---

[26] 110 Squadron was also the first unit to receive the DH9A with 18 Westland-produced aircraft delivered to the squadron in August 1918. These aircraft were financed by His Serene Highness, the Nizam of Hyderabad in support of the war effort. In recognition of this, each aircraft was marked with an inscription either side of the nose to read "Presented by his Highness the Nizam of Hyderabad, Hyderabad No......" with the individual number 1-18 (excepting that No. 13 was replaced by 12A, a concession to superstition). From this time, the squadron was officially titled No.110 (Hyderabad) Squadron, and Nizams' crest which depicted a half-tiger was incorporated into the squadron badge.

fighter attacks and so, only five aircraft returned. Secondly, on 5 October, thirteen 110 Squadron DH.9As launched to attack Cologne, with secondary and tertiary targets Coblenz and Erhang, respectively. The squadron again formed up in two close formations, flying at an altitude of 17,000 feet, however, strong westerly winds forced the formations off course and, Kaiserslautern and Pirmasens were attacked instead. The formations were under almost constant attack by German scout aircraft both outbound to the target and on return. Four DH.9A aircraft were lost to the enemy fighters. Trenchard credits this situation in his Air Ministry report writing that, "In September and October, our day bombing squadrons had to fight practically from the front line to their objective, and from there home again. In several cases they had to fight the whole way out and the whole way back". 110 Squadron lost seventeen of its aircraft between 14th September, 1918 and the end of hostilities.

The Night Bombers:

F.E. 2b - No 100 Squadron, equipped with Royal Aircraft Factory F.E. 2bs (nicknamed "Fees" by their operators), went to France on 24 March, 1917 to be employed exclusively as night bombers. Their arrival in theater preceded the Independent Force by over a year and as the first R.F.C. night bombers, they experimented with night operations. In truth, by this time, with the development of machine-gun interrupter systems for through-propeller firing, the F.E. 2b was obsolete. Additionally, by the standards of emerging enemy scout aircraft, it was too slow and insufficiently maneuverable to be a fighter. However, at night, these shortcomings were not critical and, serendipitously, the unrestricted forward position of the observer provided a good platform for bomb aiming. The F.E. 2b was also small and relatively agile at slow speeds and might avoid or dodge out of search light beams but it also provided a very stable platform for bombing. Major James McCudden VC, WW I fighter ace with 57-victories in single seat fighter aircraft such as the S.E. 5A, flew the F.E. 2b early in his R.F.C. flying career and said of the aircraft that, *"it was a wonderful machine, and the way our observers and pilots used to climb round the capricious nacelle was most amusing. In fact, on patrol, up high, I sometimes stood on my seat and looked over the tail, the machine was so steady and stable. My observer never liked this part of the performance, especially when one day I was doing it and one of my gloves blew off into the propeller, which* *shed a blade, and very nearly wrecked the machine before I could reach my seat and throttle my engine down."* Painted dull black as a night bomber, certainly, the F.E. 2b was not unfitted for the night bombing role and with the Independent Force, it was a very successful bombing component. It had a maximum speed of 91.5 mph, (147 km/h) at sea level, an endurance of 3 hours and a service ceiling of 11,000 ft. (3,353 m); it could carry up to 517 lb (235 kg) of bombs, which was quite impressive. Bomb loads might be 3 x 112 lb HE bombs or 1 x 230 lb HE bomb with 8 x 25 lb Cooper bombs. No. 100 Squadron under the Independent Force was based at Ochey, France and operated its F.E. 2b aircraft until late August 1918. Conversion to Handley Page O/400 began on 13 August and during the conversion process, the Squadron was able to continue some F.E. 2b bombing raids with the last on the night 22/23 August. The "Fee" evidently won the strong affection and respect of some of its aircrew such that, for example, experienced 100 Squadron observer, Lieutenant Roy Shillinglaw, responded to the suggestion that he must have been pleased to exchange the F.E. 2b for the Handley Page O/400s by responding, *"Oh no! We didn't want the Handleys! The Fees were nippy. We could slip out of a searchlight beam or the track of a Flaming Onion, we'd have time to circle a target. I was a pretty good shot then, and I reckoned I could drop a bomb in a barrel from a Fee!"* However, squadron pilot Lieutenant A. R (Reg). Kingsford (author of *"Night Raiders of the Air"*) was more qualified noting that, compared to the F.E. 2b, the Handley Page was "like driving a motor lorry after a Baby Austin." He said that although the Handley Page's control agility was so ponderous in the air that they could be *"devils"* when trying to escape an enemy searchlight beam he believed, nevertheless, that they were otherwise "great." Last word on this to the commander of 100 Squadron Maj C. Gordon Burge at the time of the cessation of hostilities and who was able to look back and say that the F.E. 2b was "a most excellent machine for night bombing," and it had performed "magnificent work".

Handley Page O/400 – The prototype Handley Page aircraft was rolled out of the factory shed on 9 December, 1915 as a design in response to an Admiralty specification that called for a heavy bomber having a wingspan of 114 feet, two 150 h.p. (110 kW) Sunbeam engines and the ability to carry six 100 lb bombs. The aircraft fitted the description of being the "bloody paralyser" anecdotally attributed the Director of the Royal Navy Air Department, Captain Murray Sueter, as he badgered the Handley Page Chief Designer for a 'game changer', and prompted by Commander Charles R. Samson who, after 1914 operational service on French and Belgian frontiers, had advised Sueter of the need for a new big bomber using this colorful descriptive expression for impactful emphasis. Designated the type 'O', it first flew on 17 December, 1915 and at that time it was the largest aircraft that had been built in Britain and was also one of the largest in the world. Such was the impression made by the Type 'O' on popular imagination that for years after World War I any large aircraft was often referred to as a "Handley Page". Not unsurprisingly, many development challenges were encountered requiring redesign of structure and other configuration changes and it was not until late 1916 that the first production O/100 models (the '100' came from the wingspan which was 100 ft) were deployed to France. Handley Page aircraft became operational in early 1917. The vulnerability to fighter attack was quickly recognized and operations were shifted to strategic night bombing particularly on German-occupied Belgian ports, railways and airfields. The Royal Air Force (R.A.F.) stood up on 1 April, 1918 and the Independent Force was established under the command of Major-General Trenchard on 6 June for strategic bombing operations against Germany. Various Handley Page units transferred to the R.A.F. under new squadron designations and were enlisted into the Independent Force. The O/100s (46 were produced) were superseded by the O/400 with the principal change being the re-engining with the more powerful 360 h.p. (270 kW) Rolls-Royce Eagle VIII engines. Additional changes included strengthened fuselage, larger bomb load, new fuel tanks and aerodynamic improvements to reduce parasite drag to increase speed and operating ceiling. Of the 549 O/400s built, over 400 were delivered before the end of hostilities. Other details are included in earlier Appendix C text including the aircraft cutaway diagram.

In a footnote to the aircraft of the Independent Force, it should be noted that one is missing. The Independent Force was established under an Air Ministry mandate to conduct strategic bombing, however, GoC Independent Force chose to amend this and to make enemy aerodromes a priority target. Indeed, of the 550 tons of bombs dropped, over 220 ¼ tons were on aerodromes. His reasoning for this is considered later, however, since part of his goal was to destroy enemy aircraft on the ground, taking off or landing as part of enemy aerodrome suppression, Trenchard sought to incorporate a scout-fighter squadron in the Independent Force mainly for escort but also potentially, for enemy aerodrome suppression. No. 45 Squadron flying Sopwith Camels (figure 33), had operated on the Austro-Italian front from the end of 1917 conducting ground attack and offensive patrols. By mid-1918, the Camel was outclassed in performance by the latest German fighters such as the Fokker D.VIII. However, it remained viable as a

Figure 33: No. 45 Squadron Sopwith Camel Scout/Fighter) Aircraft (© IWM Q 26582)

ground-attack aircraft employing 25 lb (11 kg) Cooper bombs, low-level strafing runs and the agility to execute more clinical anti-aircraft attacks.

No. 45 Squadron joined the Independent Force on 22 September, 1918. It was awaiting conversion to the superior Sopwith Snipe aircraft whose modified endurance of four and a half hours would allow it to mount viable escort duty for the day-bombers. However, the new aircraft did not arrive before the end of hostilities and Trenchard chose to limit the squadron to 'Line patrols' to suppress Hannover CL. IIIa strafing raids and Rumpler C.IV reconnaissance overflights. In his report to Weir he wrote that, without the more capable replacement Sopwith Snipes, 45 Squadron "was only used for attacking individual hostile machines which crossed our lines". The squadron lost one Camel in operations. One notable 45 Squadron pilot was John W. Pinder. Pinder had joined the R.N.A.S. aged eighteen in 1916, serving in No. 9 and 13 Squadrons becoming an ace with six aerial victories by the end of December 1917. No. 13 Squadron R.N.A.S., became 213 Squadron R.A.F. on 1 April, 1918 and Lieutenant Pinder became Captain Pinder, R.A.F. Posted to 45 Squadron in October with twelve victories and the award of the Distinguished Service Cross, during the seven remaining weeks of war, he brought down five further enemy aircraft. One of these aerial victories was a two-seat Rumpler reconnaissance aircraft on 19 October which he brought down over Xaffévillers Aerodrome.

Trenchard's offensive policy between June and November 1918 resulted in such high aircrew losses that his day squadrons, 99, 104, and 110, needed to take repeated stand-downs from operations. He noted this in private diary entry for 18 August, 1918 with "None of the day bombing squadrons are working at present owing to the shortage of pilots and machines." The exception was 55 Squadron, even though during the period July through September its aircrew losses totaled a staggering 125 percent of strength. 55 Squadron brought around eight months of day bombing experience when it was inducted into the Independent Force in June 1918. DH.4, 9 and 9A daylight raiding survivability, when attacked by fighters, depended heavily on the discipline and ability of their pilots to maintain tight formation in order to concentrate defensive fire and this ability was linked directly to operational experience. It is likely that 55 Squadron's earlier operational experience sustained a sufficient core within the squadron to continue operations despite the corrosive dilution of operational experience as recently qualified aircrew replaced the losses. Sharing the aerodrome at Ochey with 55 Squadron was 100 Squadron. A 100 Squadron pilot, 2nd Lieutenant A.R. Kingsford admiringly wrote[27] that "55 had been having a bad spin, losing machines day after day, but they never wavered. . . . They were flying D.H.4s and really needed escorts, for the Hun scouts gave them a bad time". A further example of the circumstances that led to the stand-downs of the day squadrons is the 31 July, 1918, raid on Mainz by twelve 99 Squadron D.H.9s. The aircraft took off at 05:30 and, even before the trench lines were crossed, three aircraft aborted their attack with engine problems. The remaining nine took up defensive-wedge formations and continued until they approached Saarbrücken where they were attacked from above and below by an estimated forty German fighters. Assessing the situation, the mission commander decided that in view of the overwhelming enemy resistance, it would be impossible to reach their original objective and so he changed the target to Saarbrücken. Four DH.9 aircraft were shot down before they reached the new target but the five remaining aircraft pressed on, reached and bombed the Saarbrücken railway junction. The D.H.9s turned for home and three more DH.9s were brought down. Only two D.H.9 aircraft made a safe recovery. Fourteen squadron aircrew were lost with five

---

[27] From his book, "Night Raiders of the Air"

KIA and nine taken as prisoners of war. The effect of this loss necessitated the aforementioned squadron stand down from operations pending the arrival of replacement aircrew. It should also be recalled that the DH.9 with its lower 200 h.p. output supported too low an altitude ceiling for formatting long-distance daylight interdiction operations and too little power for adequate station keeping. 99 Squadron was withdrawn from operations 1 to18 August to re-group, receive more aircraft and to conduct operational formation practice. 99 Squadron's twin burden of mediocre DH.9 aircraft and operationally inexperienced aircrew were not difficulties to be easily overcome and resuming operations, during the remainder of August, the squadron was able to mount just six further missions. The weight on aircrew nerves was evidently heavy and a number were suffering from "flying fatigue" and although "unwell for several weeks, (but) had continued their flying duties, and avoided the Medical Officer" until replacement aircrew arrived to relieve them.

No. 104 Squadron, flying the inferior DH.9, sustained 134 aircrew losses from June until November 1918 and was forced to stand-down three times because of this – indeed, from 6 June until 8 July, it actually lost over half its members. No. 110 (Hyderabad) Squadron, flying DH.9A flew its first Independent Force mission on 14 September, 1918 and during the period to 10 November, the squadron was forced to stand down twice as a result of debilitating aircrew losses.

DH aircraft aircrew sick-reporting increased along with combat losses. It was not solely related to symptoms of "flying fatigue" but also physiological due to high-altitude (15,000 – 18,000 feet) respiratory ailments and frostbite. The attrition of the day bombing squadrons mounted but Trenchard appeared to have given little priority to developing a coherent strategic bombing policy that was either consonant with Sykes' instructions or that weighed his squadron losses against the value of destruction caused to the enemy war effort. Indeed, his opposition to the principle of strategic bombing was unwavering as he called for more effort from his squadrons to attack targets that impacted the enemy's ability to fight and were directly associated with the B.E.F., French or American ground operations and that most strongly supported his continued independence from Air Ministry command structure. He appeared to remain irrevocably committed to sending out his squadrons despite the losses in a seemingly personal ad hoc air campaign that only halted when this squadron or that, ran out of aircrew or serviceable aircraft. In September, 1918 Trenchard visited 110 Squadron at its home Bettoncourt Aerodrome to give a pep-talk to the aircrew.

Prior to Trenchard's Bettoncourt visit, 110 Squadron had become privy to up-coming headquarte'rs proposals to bomb deeper into enemy territory in the Ruhr Valley and to targets such as Essen. While resistant to Sykes' strategic bombing directive, Trenchard certainly saw value in bombing that might undermine German morale and, indeed, in a 23 June, 1918 report to Weir, he pandered to his strategic bombing orders writing, "It must be remembered that the morale effect at present is far greater than the material effect, so it is of the utmost importance to utilize to the utmost both morale and material effect. It is more often the morale effect that makes the enemy immobilize a large number of his means of warfare such as aeroplanes and Anti-Aircraft Guns than material effect." By September, he seems to have become somewhat obsessed with the value to be gained by bombing "special long distance" targets that he believed would achieve significant impact on German morale in addition to the tactical aerodrome and railway targets which were in direct defiance of Sykes' instructions. He chose targets in the Ruhr Valley such as the Essen Krupp's Works, which required long range flights.

The observers in 110 Squadron did their calculations and concluded that their DH.9A aircraft did not carry sufficient petrol to get to an Essen target and back. It was unsettling news. Gathered round and standing smartly to attention, Trenchard told them that they would be bombing Essen. He added the encouragement that, "Of course some of you may not get back". A witness to the occasion noted that as a motivational message, "This did not go down well." As operations began again, 110 Squadron did not reach Essen and the Ruhr Valley or, indeed, Cologne to the south of these industrial locations. Their high casualty rates against long-range targets deeper in Germany demonstrated clearly that sustained attacks by daylight were materially too expensive to be sustained by the Independent Force.

Taken together, all of the Independent Force day-squadron losses due to combat or accident wastage during the period June-November 1918 averaged 12.5 aircraft per month, per squadron. Since the DH squadrons were 18-aircraft units, the monthly loss rate was an incredible 70%. Perhaps by mid-1918, the wastage of men and material immunized leadership to accept losses with little curiosity or need for accountability; attritional air-fighting was ubiquitous, acceptable and the norm. Following the 31 July losses sustained by 99 Squadron, Trenchard ciphered the Air Ministry with the message, *Regret to inform you that No. 99 Squadron (B.H.P. D.H.9) . . . lost seven machines. Only two returned. . . . Utmost importance to make this*

Squadron up to strength. Can special effort be made." Apparently there was no inquiry into the loss of the seven aircraft and aircrews that set out to attack Mainz but actually attacked a secondary target, Saarbrücken because of the intensity of enemy attacks. Was Saarbrücken railway junction really worth the losses? As a target, it certainly did not appear to conform to Sykes's direction for Independent Force strategic bombing. Furthermore, Trenchard's use of his squadrons appears unscientific with a level of wastage that can only be described as being profligate. It was attritional aerial warfighting that became a count-down to near-zero aircraft and aircrew leading to periodic squadron stand-downs and was simply not sustainable over time.

With regard to the night operations, in his January 1919 final report to Weir, Trenchard draws a contrast with day bombing and writes "night bombing is safer (but) many mistakes are made at night in reaching the locality it has been decided to bomb." The reasons for the difficulty in reaching target locations were that navigational aids were limited in capability, replacement aircrew were inexperienced, adverse weather might have a massive impact on aircraft course, speed and control and, dead-reckoning (DR) navigation with all of its vagaries, was not an assured way to find a target cloaked in cloud and darkness. Various strategies were adopted to redress these challenges, and Handley Page night raids would of preference be timed to coincide with the week-long periods of full moons. For example, September 1918's moon waxed on 16/17, with fifty percent of full-moon brightness, and ended on the evening of 23/24 providing a conducive mission window of 16/17 – 23/24 September. However, the effect of all of these things meant that finding targets, in large part, was a matter of luck; in regard to the matter of safety, actually, night operations were certainly more demanding and dangerous to fly than flights by day insofar as the risk of accidents and associated aircrew casualties was statistically around double that for day operations. Whatever the case, the introduction of the Handley Page O/400 as an Independent Force night bomber with an ability to carry a 2,000 lb (907 kg) bomb load altered the balance in value of day compared to night bombing. Each Handley Page squadron comprised ten aircraft, usually with six committed to a night's operations. A Handley Page squadron might carry around four times the bomb load of a DH squadron.

The Handley Page squadron losses, spread across the five Independent Force squadrons, fell well short of the day squadron losses. A measure of this is that none of the Handley Page squadrons required a formal stand-down from combat operations. The following table shows the losses in the night operating squadrons during the period June through the November Armistice. It is abundantly clear that the August ramp-up with 97, 215 and 115 squadrons joining 216 on the Independent Force strength and 99 beginning conversion to Handley Pages, that September became the time when Trenchard chose to demonstrate the value of his bombing command. The addition of the new squadrons and conversion of 99 Squadron to DH.9A aircraft essentially tripled the weight of bombs that the Independent Force could deliver in a day-night period and in September the weight of bombs dropped during the night hours was the nearly the same as the previous two months added together. The cost in aircrew losses of the September night operations is shocking and suggests that the Handley Page squadrons were either ill prepared or used in a way that was operationally unsuitable. 215 Squadron was particularly affected and it sustained losses of 93.3% of squadron strength in this single month alone.

The missions that Independent Force headquarters tasked became quite eclectic and far removed from the strategic target set identified by Sykes's Air Staff. Trenchard was particularly focused on enemy aerodromes, railway junctions and rail rolling stock, which was in critical short supply. With regard to the first of these, the enemy aerodromes, he made the argument in his final report to Weir that, "before it was possible to attack Germany successfully it was necessary to attack the enemy's aerodromes heavily in order to prevent his attacking our aerodromes by night, and by destroying his machines, to render his attacks by day less efficacious". He anticipated that his attacks on aerodromes by his Independent Force might ultimately take up half of his bombing effort (had the war extended into 1919) and justified the attacks by reason of the "necessity of preventing the enemy's bombing machines attacking our aerodromes and in order to destroy large numbers of the enemy's scouts on their aerodromes." He further argued that the large effort expended on the enemy aerodromes was "thoroughly justified when it is taken into consideration that the enemy's attacks on our aerodromes were practically negligible, and not a single machine was destroyed by bombing during the period June 5th to Nov. 11th." What is not said is how many aircraft were lost in the raids on German aerodromes in order to achieve the contended freedom from attack of his own aerodromes – actually, eight enemy attacks were made on Independent Force aerodromes between 12 July and 26 September and these caused little damage. Although Trenchard implies that the credit for his Independent Force aerodrome immunity from significant enemy attacks belongs to his German aerodrome bombing campaign, in actuality, there appear few facts to support the contention. Post-war German accounts did not appear to support a case that

Independent Force Night Bomber Squadron Casualties, June – November, 1918

100 Squadron

Month		KIA	WIA	MIA	Total		% Squadron Strength
June		0	1	0	1		3.3%
July		0	0	0	0		0
August		0	0	0	0		0
September		0	0	2	2		6.7%
October		1	2	0	3		10.0%
November		0	0	0	0		0
	Total	1	3	2	6		20%

216 Squadron

Month		KIA	WIA	MIA	Total		% Squadron Strength
June		0	0	0	0		0
July		0	0	3	3		10.0%
August		0	0	0	0		0
September		0	3	3	6		20%
October		0	0	0	0		0
November		0	0	0	0		0
	Total	0	3	6	9		30%

97 Squadron

Month		KIA	WIA	MIA	Total		% Squadron Strength
August		1	0	9	10		33.3%
September		1	1	0	2		6.7%
October		0	0	0	0		0
November		0	0	0	0		0
	Total	2	1	9	12		40%

215 Squadron

Month		KIA	WIA	MIA	Total		% Squadron Strength
August		0	1	3	4		13.3%
September		2	1	25	28		93.3%
October		0	1	3	4		13.3%
November		0	0	0	0		0
	Total	2	3	31	36		120%

115 Squadron

Month		KIA	WIA	MIA	Total		% Squadron Strength
September		0	1	3	4		13.3%
October		0	0	0	0		0
November		0	0	0	0		0
	Total	0	1	3	4		13.3%

Figures taken from "Biplanes and Bombsights, British Bombing in World War I" by G.K. Williams bombing these aerodromes was significantly consequential. Additionally, an VIII Brigade intelligence report[28] based on inspections of airfields such as Morhange, Boulay, Buhl, Frescaty and Folpersweiler that were conducted after the Armistice concluded that, "On the whole one is forced to believe that, except on rare occasions, the actual destruction of hangars and installations has been moderate. But on the other hand, the material damage to the actual machines has been great." By arguing his need to attack German aerodromes in order to protect his own aerodromes and, thereby, stray from the Air Ministry direction that the Independent Force mission was solely to bomb strategic targets, Trenchard chose an argument that sounded plausibly authentic, however, it appears to be an imposter since the actual degree of damage inflicted on German aerodromes did not rise to a level that supports the contention that this bombing was responsible for disabling an enemy response.

If the material damage to enemy aerodromes was unlikely to be the comprehensive reason that was responsible for stopping German night bombers raiding his aerodromes, Trenchard could make a stronger case for bombing to destroy enemy scout aircraft on the ground and thereby help protect his DH aircraft. His day squadrons continued to sustain heavy casualties from attacking enemy scout aircraft until the end of hostilities and, other than 45 Squadron, he was unable to mount effective fighter escort cover to protect them. By bombing enemy scout aircraft, which were evidently numerous and a real and present threat to the survival of Independent Force day bomber aircraft and crews, he had a practical a way to attrit the enemy's ability to continue their attacks. While not being specific on the source, the 'Report on the Effects and Results of the Bombing of Germany by 8th Brigade and Independent Force' suggests, "that on average two (enemy) machines were damaged as a result of each raid" from bomb splinters. The credit that Trenchard takes for the bombing offensive against the aerodromes is stated to be "thoroughly justified when taken into consideration that the enemy's attacks (by German night bombers) were practically negligible", however, he is less forthcoming about the continued German scout attacks that assailed his day bombers until the end of the war. This begs the question, if the destruction of German night bombers was so thoroughly complete as a result of aerodrome bombing, why then were so many scouts not similarly destroyed – and surely the enemy scouts were the

---

[28] Report on the Effects and Results of the Bombing of Germany by 8th Brigade and Independent Force, Royal Air Force: (D) Aerodromes

greatest of the airborne threats to the Independent Force DH.4/9/9As? It is hard not to conclude that the bombing of German airfields was less successful than is claimed by Trenchard and, if this is so, the loss in day and night bombers, half a squadron lost in some raids with an "average" of only two enemy machines damaged, seems to be poor material return (let alone the human cost).

H.A. Jones, in his treatise "The War in the Air"[29], conjectures, "It may be that too great a proportion of activities of the bombing squadrons was directed against aerodrome targets," and that the failing German logistics and the paucity of aircraft replacements were otherwise diminishing whatever enemy capability to bomb the Independent Force aerodromes at night actually existed. Trenchard might have hesitated and taken stock and only bombed enemy aerodromes if they proved to be active in bombing his airfields. In this way, he might have reduced his high losses on aerodrome attacks or, leastways, have preserved his aircraft and experienced aircrews for the strategic missions. However, Jones acknowledges Trenchard's character, writing, "It was never his way...to let the enemy dictate his policy." Whether it was Weir or Sykes or the French or the weather...or the enemy, Trenchard followed his own robust and instinctive dictates in respect of enemy aerodrome bombing; undoubtedly, the aerial war effort with the Independent Force was his alone to dictate.

---

[29] "The War in the Air: being The Story of the Part Played in the Great War by the Royal Air Force" Is an official history based -mainly on records made available by the Air Ministry, supplemented by a variety of other sources, experts and eyewitnesses. Six volumes and supporting appendices were produced and published between 1922 and 1937. The work was begun by Walter Raleigh who completed the first volume and died shortly after it was published. The task of completing the tome was taken up by H.A Jones.

Before considering the other targets that Trenchard decided to attack, it is worthwhile to reprise what were his bombing orders and how he interpreted them. On 20 June, 1918, Trenchard issued Operational Order No. 1 to his Independent Force squadrons and staffs (see table below). In it, he incorporated the non-strategic targets of railways and aerodromes, counter to Air Ministry orders. His VIII Brigade predecessor and subsequent deputy of the Independent Force, Newall, had written a report titled, "The Scientific and Methodical Attack of Vital Industries" on 27 May, 1918. This report was prior to Trenchard's arrival and it identified a set of enemy targets having strategic war value. It seems likely that Trenchard took Newall's report and adapted it before sending it to Weir on 23 June, 1918 as formal report titled "Memorandum on the Tactics to be Adopted in Bombing the Industrial Centres of Germany." Trenchard made changes to the listing priority of

Independent Force Targets – Informed to Squadrons and Air Minister			
Priority	Trenchard's 20 June 1918 Operational Order 1	Trenchard's 23 June 1918 Memorandum Paper to Weir	Newall's 27 May Paper- adapted by Trenchard
1	Chemical Works	Chemical Works	Iron and Coal Mines
2	Iron and Steel Works	Iron and Steel Works	Blast Furnaces
3	Railways	Aero Engine/Magneto Works	Chemical Production
4	Aero Engine Works	Submarine/Shipbuilding Works	Explosive Production
5	Aerodromes	Large Gun Shops	Miscellaneous Production - Railway Material, Rolling Stock, Aircraft, Internal Combustion Engines, Submarine Parts, Magneto and Tanning Industries
6		Engine Repair Shops	

targets that Newall identified and, in his paper to Weir, he made no mention of the tactical railway and aerodrome targets that feature in his Operational Order of 20 June. He evidently concealed his intention to bomb aerodromes and railways from the Minister since the strategic targets that he advised to Weir were military objectives that were certainly not the same as he ordered his squadrons commanders to attack in the written orders of 20 June.

119

And where practice overtakes precept, such that Trenchard flaunted his strategic bombing mandate (which seems to be rather incredible in modern day retrospect), evidentially, for example, his Operation orders to his squadrons for most of the month of July almost exclusively designate enemy aerodromes as the principal raiding targets. Although Sykes had prohibited the use of Independent Force bomber assets for strategic reconnaissance or attacks on enemy aerodromes and railways, in late June, Trenchard withdrew aircraft from bombing operations in order to conduct reconnaissance of the German rail networks around Thionville and Saarbrücken.

Trenchard undoubtedly sensed some need to cover his tracks in order to defend his selection of targets from censure by the Air Staff or Sykes. If the enemy was producing poison gas at a chemical works, then trains and the rail network were required to take gas shells to the front lines. So, while he would raid the chemical works that were classified as bona fide strategic targets in his orders, he would argue that by stopping the means of transport by destroying the railway centers, he would achieve the same end. In his Air Staff memorandum, "Order of Importance and Types of Targets and Reasons for Importance"[30] of 15 October, 1918, he explained this view as, "raids can be carried out on some of the most important chemical and railway centres with a view to, if possible, reducing the output" to the enemy front line. In this way, he was able to merge his strategic and tactical attack reasoning and perhaps, provide a hedge in any need to defend his bombing focus on the railway network. In fact, his reasoning here is very similar to the argument used in support of his aerodrome offensive. The Independent Force preponderance of effort of aerodromes and railways between June and August is illustrated in the next figures:

	June	July	August
Aerodromes	13.3%	28.0%	49.5%
Railways	55.0%	46.0%	31.0%
Total	68.3%	74.0%	80.5%

[30] In the 15 October memorandum, Trenchard lists the classes of bombing targets to include "Chemical, Poison Gas, Explosive, Munition, Powder Works, Aviation, Blast Furnaces, and Railway Stations." Further decomposed these objectives are not prioritized and he reserves the detail choice to the "Commander of the Force", in this case himself, who must only consider such objectives as simply the broad policy on which to "base his bombing programme." Essentially, this paper provides a further attempt in the defense of his aerodrome and railway bombing campaign policy.

The Air Staffs were well aware that Trenchard was concentrating on railways and aerodromes and not on strategic enemy core industries, the raison d'être of the Independent Force. However, it appears that they were simply powerless to change Trenchard's direction. It is not clear why Sykes was unwilling to confront his subordinate. Sykes's Air Ministry staffs continued to draw their Commander's attention to Trenchard's neglect of the strategic bombing directive and yet he chose to do nothing – was he simply afraid of Trenchard or had Weir made it clear to him that his own arrangement gave Trenchard *droit du seigneur* to act without accountability to Sykes? Certainly, his departmental Air Staff[31], with responsibility for Independent Force matters, reported the situation and were frustrated by the ongoing situation. In a long memorandum to Sykes on 11 September, 1918, Deputy Chief of the Air Staff, Brig Gen P. R. C. Groves[32] reported that Air Staff Independent Force targeting policy was being ignored by Trenchard. He summed it up by saying, "I would submit that the policy pursued at present amounts to the diversion of maximum effort against targets of subsidiary importance. Such a dissipation of Air Force is at variance with the policy laid down by the Air Council in the above-mentioned letter (Secretarial Letter No. 11555/1918, 13 May, 1918) and with the views put forward by you in the declared policy of the Air Staff submitted to the War Cabinet in a printed paper on June 17th." While sympathetic to the argument made by Groves that Independent Force offensive operations should be brought into line with Air Ministry policy, Sykes took no effective action to make it so.

The frustration of the Air Staff Directorate of Flight Operations (DFO) increased with the mounting conviction that too many Independent Force bombing attacks were being made on enemy "railway objectives which are placed by the Air Staff as third in order of importance on the priority list of targets" and because it was for the destruction of strategic targets (industries) that the Independent Force was established. However, not only were the wrong targets being attacked but the losses of aircraft and aircrew were exceedingly heavy. Writing an internal report dated 17 September,

---

[31] Two groups were established in the Air Directorate with responsibility to support strategic bombing – the first being the F03 Branch, Strategic Bombing and Independent Force Operations, within the Directorate of Flying Operations and the second, the AI 1B Section, within the Directorate of Air Intelligence Bomb Raids and Targets, AI 1Branch, Receipt and Distribution of Intelligence.

[32] Brig Gen P. R. C. Groves became Deputy Chief of the Air Staff on 1 April, 1918, replacing Major-General M E F Kerr who fell awry of General Trenchard. Formerly a Navy officer, he transferred to the Royal Air Force in 1918. He was killed in a flying accident in 1920 aged 40 whilst serving in Egypt.

1918, citing figures submitted by Trenchard's staff, the Air Staff Directorate of Flight Operations (DFO), Staff Officer Captain H. McClelland, D.S.C.[33], reported that flying hours in July had risen by 33% but the number of aircraft lost had increased by 67%. For August, compared with July, flying hours had increased by a further 13% but at cost of a 31% increase in aircraft lost. Losses rose at twice the rate of flying hours and were rapidly diluting the core of experienced aircrew. In one of those curious cases of irony, because most enemy aerodromes and railways were close to the Lines and, therefore, most easily found by replacement inexperienced aircrew, Trenchard found that the circumstance of diminishing experienced aircrew in the air (e.g. navigation) supported the choice for his tactical bombing offensive, mainly against rail and aerodrome targets. For example, the sprawling Metz-Sablon 'rail triangle' was located only 12 miles behind the trenches and inexperienced aircrews could find at night and identify their objectives and bomb them without getting lost out or in-bound. However, not only was the Independent Force not attacking strategic targets but the losses that were being sustained seemed to many to be outweighing the material damage being done to the enemy. The ebullient Trenchard invariably reported raid successes, however, the scale of losses raised questions for anyone paying attention. It was not just the Air Staffs who were disturbed about Trenchard's personal campaign. Confiding to his diary, Maj W. R. Read, Commanding Officer 216 Squadron considered the balance of losses against achievement as, "if a squadron does a great deal of work without losing many machines it is doing as good work as a Squadron that is doing slightly better work but at a high cost of machines and personnel." As for day bombing, even with the more powerful and reliable Liberty engines, the DH 9A aircraft of 110 squadron were unable to reach strategic more distant targets with any consistency and without incurring unacceptable aircraft and aircrew losses.

In his last defence to Weir, Trenchard observed that "it was necessary several times during the period of the (Independent) operation to

---

[33] Captain McClelland joined Directorate of Flight Operations FO3 in June 1918 and stayed there until the Armistice. His tasks included "analysis and filing of all reports and records. Circulation and summaries & c., of operations of Independent Force. War Diary of Independent Force." When he took up his appointment in FO3, he likely possessed more night and long-range bombing experience than anyone on the Air Staff. He had commanded the first group to deploy to France as part of Newall's 41st Wing in October 1917 and he flew in the first mission on 24/25 October, 1917 to attack the Burbach wire-rolling mill at Saarbrücken. On 24/25 March, 1918, McClelland commanded one of two Handley Pages which took off to raid Cologne. However, after crossing the lines, his engines boiled and he was forced to return. A second start was made and, when near Metz, one of the engines cut out entirely. Nevertheless, he dropped his bombs at railway at Courcelles and returned on one engine. McClelland was an impressive operator and certainly one to be listened to…if not contemporaneously, certainly by history.

carry out attacks in conjunction with the (Allied) Armies on the enemy's communications". With the arrival of early September 1918, the Franco-American offensive on the St. Mihiel Salient began. At the request of the Allies, Trenchard turned his attention and diverted the Independent Force in support of Allied army ground operations. Initially, adverse weather limited Independent Force bombing operations but, between 12-17 September, attacks were mounted against aerodromes and railways, the latter in particular on the Metz-Sablon railway triangle which was important for enemy logistic supply to St. Mihiel – in support of the St. Mihiel offensive, it is notable that the Allies brought together the largest ever, at that time, air concentration involving 1,481 aircraft, mainly French and British aircraft. Later in the month, Franco-American forces launched another offensive between Rheims and Verdun and known as the Meuse-Argonne Offensive. Also known as the Battle of the Argonne Forest, it was part of the overall Allied offensive along the Western Front lasting from 26 September, 1918 until the Armistice. From 23 to 27 September, the Independent Force again supported the Meuse-Argonne ground offensive.

Trenchard made some concessions to the broader value of strategic raids, which, to be effective, required precision bombing. He believed in the preeminence of damaging enemy morale as an effective tool of war, which possibly was a lesson that he had learned from the South African Boer War (along with Smuts from the other side) when the Boer guerrillas' success was undermined by the internment of civilians in concentration camps. In his later and last memorandum to Weir, he qualified his belief writing, "the moral(e) effect of bombing stands undoubtedly to the material effect in a proportion of 20 to 1, and therefore it was necessary to create the greatest moral(e) effect possible". As noted earlier in these writings, he also recognized that the size and technical capability of his Independent Force was insufficient to allow the bombing intensity necessary to cause comprehensive damage to a significant number enemy works or centres of population. With the squadrons at his disposal, his predilection for damaging enemy morale might be achieved, he believed, with the choice to either concentrate his bombers on a very few targets and seek to inflict extensive damage or to raid many targets on very few occasions causing only limited damage but sowing the seeds of uncertainty. He decided on the latter. He wrote that by focusing on only one or two enemy towns, "all the other towns are feeling fairly safe." So, with those of his Independent Force not engaged in bombing airfields or railways, he conducted an additional distributed aerial-bombing campaign anticipating that the uncertainty of where bombs might fall would wither enemy civilian morale and their will to stay in the fight. Trenchard's targeting of enemy morale was outside the Independent Force stated strategic bombing mandate and, of course, success would in any case have been difficult to prove. He could claim that German morale was damaged and be beyond contradiction from his critics – without clear metrics, who could prove otherwise? Furthermore, wherever bombs fell, so long as behind the Western Front and in enemy territory, he could claim relevance as part of an assault on enemy morale. This strategy diluted the limited aircraft and crew resources at his disposal and, contrary to a more technical convention for strategic bombing (i.e. making precision bombing targets a top priority), it placed focus on the destruction of war-supporting material behind an effort to damage enemy morale by terror bombing the civilian population. If not in synch with Sykes, it certainly seems to have been with Weir. Writing to Trenchard in September 1918, Weir wrote that he "would very much like it if (Trenchard) could start up a really big fire in one of the German towns. ... I can conceive of nothing more terrifying to a civilian population as bombing from a low altitude, and I was frequently very apprehensive that the Bosch[e] would do this in London, and that the results would be very serious." He went on to suggest, "If I were you, I would not be too exacting as regards accuracy in bombing railway stations in the middle of towns[34]. The enemy is susceptible to bloodiness, and I would not mind a few accidents due to inaccuracy". In his reply, Trenchard was able to say that inaccuracy was much the norm for the Independent Force bombers and that he thought Weir need not be "anxious about our degree of accuracy when bombing stations in the middle of towns. The accuracy is not great at present, and all the pilots drop their eggs well into the middle of the town generally." While he initially eschewed the bombing of civilian complexes in favour of strategic material targets, which demanded precision bombing to be effective, Sykes, possibly bending to Weir and the War Cabinet and to the

---

[34] If Weir was not too fussy about who was killed – non-combatant men, women and children - so long as they were German, in what was essentially his direct encouragement of 'terror bombing', the same was perhaps less true of Independent Force aircrew. 100 Squadron F.E. 2b Observer, 2nd Lieutenant Roy Shillinglaw felt able to say, "I don't think that anybody deliberately bombed civilian houses or civilian people as far as my colleagues and myself were concerned. We were very, very keen to be on our targets...." Shillinglaw recognized that collateral damage could and did occur and that it likely was "demoralizing to some of the civilian inhabitants" but that this was not a mission objective, so far as he was concerned. This does not appear to be the personal view of one noble aviator either because he goes on to say, "We were very keen to be on target because our errors were shown up on those photographs (Note: post-raid damage assessment intelligence photographs), there was no kidding the authorities and I think we were pretty accurate on the whole." So, it appears that Squadron Commands were also not a party to Weir's hopes or indeed Trenchard's disinclination to disappoint him.

'tsunami' of influence that Trenchard evidently wielded, ultimately concurred that the large-scale bombing of German cities – with the express purpose of destroying enemy civilian centres - was an additional priority. Trenchard was well on his way to establishing 'area bombing' as the future raison d'être of the Royal Air Force strike – a sort of armed rehearsal.

In one of those curious happenstances, one strategic target, blast furnaces, was drawn into Trenchard's otherwise largely tactical aerial-bombing campaign simply because furnaces glowed brightly at night and, thereby, they facilitated easier recognition. Trenchard certainly had the military nous to recognize how the difficulties of adverse weather, aircraft reliability, aerial night navigation and simple overhead target recognition compromised the likelihood of achieving successful raids deep into enemy territory. Blast furnaces literally stood out alone, glowing redly in the dark of the night. Choosing the blast furnaces as second tier targets[35] (behind aerodromes and railways), he still could not hide his skepticism[36] regarding their value, despite Air Ministry priority, in writing, "they were easy to find at night, although it was difficult to do any really serious damage to them owing to the smallness of the vital part of the works".

As a brief afterthought on these distributed aerial raids, Trenchard was to assert in his diary writings that his Independent Force "attacks forced the redistribution of a disproportionate part of German air strength to home defence duties." In so doing, he purported that fighting at the front was materially eased for allied forces. This is one of those arguments that appeals, since it appears to be based on common sense and becomes widely held but is, nevertheless, false dogma. However, as Williams[37] points out in his fine analysis "Biplanes and Bombsights British Bombing in World War

---

[35] Interestingly, while the 41st Air Wing was under Newall's command and prior to his supersession by Trenchard, it conducted in excess of half its operations against blast furnaces and chemical (e.g. Soda Works) and munition works. 55 and 100 Squadrons were involved and 53.5% of Air Wing sorties involved these targets with 57.4% of bomb weight dropped. This met the strategic bombing mandate of the War Cabinet and that was anticipated to diminish the enemy ability to sustain warfare.

[36] Trenchard's skepticism was wisely founded. The supporters of strategic bombing continued to overestimate the value of aerial bombing of blast furnace complexes. Furnace sites were large and bombing appears rarely to have disabled an iron work's capability. Indeed, the results of some raids on target went unnoticed by the industrial and civilian populations. Probably the primary reason for the general failure against German blast furnaces was that they could never be attacked in the strength sufficient to deliver sufficient ordnance to achieve more complete site destruction.

[37] Quoting from a German report which notes "The number of "Kest" (Kampfeinsitzerstaffel) single seater fighter squadrons employed in home air defence could unfortunately be increased no further. Some of the squadrons in fact had to be sent to the front."

I", German home defense does not appear to have been given a high priority often having "to make do with an assortment of aging aircraft discarded by front-line fighter units[38]". However, Trenchard would have none of this writing to Weir that, from June 1918 onwards, the number of enemy (home defence) aircraft opposing the Independent Force increased and he presumed that they had been "withdrawn from the Russian Front and re-equipped for Home Defence work". This diversion of aircraft remains unproven and unlikely since German priority remained to counter the effect of America's entry into the war, which compelled the strengthening of the aerial forces over the Western Front to deal with the combined English-French-American air forces. Further, in the 1918 German reorganization of military aviation, the British strategic aerial bombardment by the Royal Air Force did not appear to attract any discrete strengthening of the their home defense aviation component. Nevertheless, whether reinforced or not, equipped with the less advanced aircraft or not, German Home Defence was a determined force and undoubtedly, fighting with the aircraft that it had, it caused the Independent Force heavy losses.

The losses of the Independent Force during its few months of operation were very high, and were characterized by several squadron stand-downs in order to recover operational cohesion (see next table). Trenchard, with his penchant to wage war in his own way, did not appear to reduce the attack tempo as, steadily, experienced aircrews were attrited and replaced by inexperienced crews, only to lead to an increased rate of loss. Sustained long-range day bombing was manifestly unsustainable to wit the losses by the DH4 and DH9/9A squadrons of the Independent Force. The day bombers of the Independent Force sustained 257 aircrew losses and 262 aircraft between June and November 1918 – rates of ~12 aircrew and ~12.5 aircraft per month, respectively. The night squadrons did not suffer the high losses of the day squadrons, save 215 Squadron (which in the month of September 1918 sustained losses of 93.3% of squadron strength) but there were no formal operational Handley Page stand-downs. It is perhaps notable that September marked the time that Trenchard's Independent Force achieved full squadron strength; however, it was largely operationally constrained to support to allied ground offensives, in so far as the adverse weather allowed. The night of 16/17 September involved a wide spread of targets (e.g.

---

[38] "British Air Policy on the Western Front, 1914-1918", by Malcolm Cooper, London ; Boston : Allen & Unwin, 1986

Cologne and Mannheim) and all five of the Handley Page squadrons were engaged in raids into enemy territory leading to the loss of ten aircraft – essentially, the equivalent of one whole squadron or 20% of the VIII Brigade night-bomber strength. This loss was obfuscated in reports of the Independent Force headquarter's staffs, however, such was the apparent shock to the Command that, during the remainder of September, the Handley Page squadrons were restricted to targets closer to home aerodromes, such as the Metz-Sablon rail triangle. This fit quite well into Trenchard's military preference for aerodromes and railways and the actuality that these represented the only classes of targets that he could hope to raid on a sustained basis; being that they lay more within the proficiency of the Independent Force replacement aircrews, less experienced at airmanship, navigation and facing weather hazards and enemy defenses.

Date	Flying Hours		Weight Bombs Dropped (tons)	Independent Force Bombing Campaign Details (Missing in Action (MIA) and Lost – Total Loss)												Notes
	Day	Night		DH 4		DH.9		DH.9A		F.E. 2b		HP O/400		Total		
				MIA	Lost	MIA	Lost	MIA	Lost	MIA	Lost	MIA	Lost	MIA	Lost	
June	1,514	399	57	3	7	6	13	-	-	-	4	-	-	9	24	Independent Force (IF) established with 55 Sqn (DH 4), 99 & 104 Sqns (DH 9), 216 HP and 100 Sqn (F.E. 2b)
July	1,768	767	88	2	6	13	22	-	-	-	10	1	3	16	41	
August	2,019	846	101	7	16	14	22	-	-	1	5	5	11	27	54	95 Sqn (H.P.) – 9 Aug – Joins IF. 215 Sqn (H.P.) – 19 Aug – Joins IF 100 Sqn (H.P.) – 13 Aug – Re-eqips 115 Sqn (H.P.) – 31 Aug – Joins IF 110 Sqn (DH 9) – 19 Aug – Joins IF
September	1,605	761	179	4	14	16	20	6	7	-	-	11	13	37	54	
October	1,828	629	98	-	7	2	13	11	21	-	-	1	18	14	59	
November	661	109	20	2	1	3	4	-	0	-	-	-	6	6	11	
Totals	9,395	3,511	543	18	52	54	94	17	28	1	19	18	51	108	243	
Overall Totals				69		148		45		20		69		351		

Independent Force flying hours, weight of ordnance dropped and aircraft losses during the period June – November 1918 (thanks to H.A. Jones, history of the Royal Air Force, World War I, "The War in the Air")

In his final report to Weir, Trenchard cited a number of Independent Force attacks, which included two particular 215 Squadron night raids that were typical of the operations conducted. The first was on the night of 25/26 August, when two aircraft from the squadron, crewed respectively by Captain W.B. Lawson (pilot) and Lieutenant S.E. Towill (observer)[39] and Lieutenant M.C. Purvis (pilot) and Lieutenant W.E. Crombie (observer), conducted an audacious attack on the Badische Anilin Soda Fabrik Works at Mannheim; it was a distance there and back from Xaffévillers of around 220 miles. This attack involved a chemical works and was evidently one that qualified as an assault on a strategic target within the definition established by the Air Ministry. Trenchard reported it as follows:

"The two machines, piloted by Captain Lawson and Lieut. Purvis, left at eight o'clock. One pilot shut off his engine at 5,000 feet and glided in on the target from the NW, following the river (Rhine). He was at once picked up and held in the beams of the searchlights, and an intense anti-aircraft barrage was put-up. The machine continuity changed its course, but could not shake off the searchlights, and the pilot was completely blinded by the glare. At this moment the second machine glided in, with its engine almost stopped, underneath the first machine, got immediately over the works, below the tops of the factory chimneys and released its bombs right into the works. The searchlights at once turned on to this machine, freeing the first machine from their glare. This machine then turned and made straight for the works as low as the second machine amongst the chimneys, and released its bombs. The searchlights were turned almost horizontally to the ground and anti-aircraft guns were firing right across the works and factories almost horizontally. In spite of this, the two machines remained at low altitude and swept the factories, works, guns and searchlights with machine-gun fire. On the return journey both of these machines passed through rain and thick clouds, whilst lightning and thunder were prevalent throughout the trip."

The second attack took place on the night of 2/3 September and involved eight 215 Squadron Handley Pages attacking Buhl aerodrome and Erhang

---

[39] Not credited here or in the Trenchard report, is that the gunlayer in this raid was Lieutenant Hugh Monaghan. Lawson and Purvis were both Canadian pilots and although himself a pilot but not scheduled to fly that night, Monaghan "volunteered to go along as gunlayer" with his fellow countrymen and was assigned to Lawson's aircraft. Lawson released the Handley Page full load of bombs at 200 ft altitude and Monaghan says that in the resulting close blast, the "plane lurched and reared but held together" but with full power on it tore away with Monaghan still "throwing Coopers overboard". He notes that in post-flight inspections, both aircraft were "badly holed" by enemy fire.

Railway Junction. Three of the Buhl aircraft conducted two bombing missions during the evening. The squadron dropped 240 bombs, amounting to a weight of over 18,500 lb of ordnance between first take-off at 19:45, 2 September and the return of the last aircraft at 01:25, 3 September. Of the first wave of six[40] whose mission was to attack Buhl, two aircraft returned with engine failure but four reached the target. The second wave launched three aircraft against Buhl, all of which successfully bombed the aerodrome. The two other aircraft raided Erhang. Both Buhl and Erhang were around a 150 mile round trip from Xaffévillers. Trenchard writes:

"On the night of 2ⁿᵈ – 3ʳᵈ September machines of No. 215 Squadron attacked Buhl aerodrome and the railway junction at Erhang, some of the machines making two trips. In the first attack on Buhl, two direct hits were obtained and three fires started, all bursts being observed on and in close proximity to the hangars. The second attack[41] was carried out from 150 to 900 feet, machines circling around the aerodrome for fifteen minutes. Excellent shooting was made and thirteen direct hits were claimed. Three hangars were entirely demolished and a fire started. In addition, motor lorries were bombed from 100 feet, and a hostile machine on the ground was attacked with good results." Sadly, it was this night that Captain G. S. Buck. MC. D.F.C. was killed when his Handley Page D5431, crashed into a petrol dump upon landing after returning from his successful raid on Erhang.

Weir's tenure as Secretary of State for Air was limited, at his own request, to the duration of the war. Weir had the responsibility to fulfill the War Cabinet intention that the Independent Force conducts a massive strategic bombing offensive against German industrial ability to wage war. He undoubtedly believed that Trenchard's earlier resignation as Chief of the Air Staff had been wrong matched by his subsequent behavior being insubordinate. However, he recognized Trenchard's key value to a nascent Royal Air Force and eventually persuaded him, despite the General's demurring turns, to take command of the Independent Force. Weir had to buy Trenchard's agreement to serve in this command by allowing him to operate independently of the new Chief of the Air Staff, Sykes, and required to report solely to him, outside normal chain of command. However, by

---

[40] 2/Lt A.C.G. Fowler piloted one of the four aircraft, D4568, successfully to reach and bomb the objective. The 'two direct hits were obtained and three fires started' referred to were the result of his aircraft's three bombing runs over the aerodrome, each at 600 feet altitude.

[41] 2/Lt A.C.G. Fowler's second mission of the night involved bombing runs at 550 feet and machine gunning airfield facilities for which he reported results credited to be "Good shooting".... "excellent shooting" according to General Trenchard.

accepting lesser Command status, which the Independent Force undoubtedly constituted when compared to his former position as Chief of Air Staff under Rothermere, Trenchard can only be described as having become a reluctant commander. During the war years, he had seen the Royal Flying Corp as an integral part of the Army under General Haig with an encompassing role of tactical support to ground operations. As Commander of the Independent Force, Trenchard was to maintain this fundamental belief and to manage his command like a private air force, largely ignoring the War Cabinet and the Air Ministry.

Weir appears to have been particularly sensitive to questions that arose that searched into whether the Independent Force was truly successful – perhaps it was because he did, in fact, realize that Trenchard, under his watch as Minister, had wandered far from the directed War-Cabinet mandate for strategic bombing. Anticipating Trenchard's final report on the Independent Force, he appears to have counselled circumspection and for Trenchard not to provide his critics with material with which to attack him; specifically in regard to his ignoring the Royal Air Force Command structure and to what degree he had fulfilled the prescribed Independent Force strategic bombardment mission. Undoubtedly, he did not wish to see, exposed to public scrutiny, Trenchard's incendiary opinion written in his private diary on 11 November that the end of the Independent Force might be welcomed as "a more gigantic waste of effort and personnel there has never been in any war." Weir saw value in Trenchard returning to the highest level of the Royal Air Force Command because of his natural standing in air force matters. Evidently, Weir sought to protect Trenchard from any self-destructive opining.

During the war years, Sykes had the clearer understanding of the value of strategic bombardment than did his "on paper" subordinate, the commander of the Independent Force. Trenchard's thinking was dominated by his predilection for tactical aerial offensive except for the contrary but very strong belief in the value of what would later become known as 'area bombing' i.e. generally indiscriminate bombardment of populated areas leading to widespread destruction as a means of eroding overall enemy morale and the continued will to fight-on by a civilian populace.

After the Armistice, Trenchard once again became Chief of the Air Staffs, an appointment that he then held for over a decade. He consolidated the independence of the Royal Air Force resisting all attempts to separate into parts that might again to serve the Navy and Army tactical needs. In this effort he was successful and earned the sobriquet of the 'Father of the Royal Air Force'. His epiphany, or was it simply political expediency[42], was to become a true convert to strategic bombing, albeit, ostensibly focused on degrading enemy morale. After all, this was consistent with the defense he advanced for his Independent Force record in which he argued that striking enemy morale compared to material damage, was in value terms in the ratio of 20:1. As Chief of the Air Staff, he proposed that the Royal Air Force could bypass ground and maritime operations and strike at the heart of the enemy's ability to support its forces in the field. The defining feature was to be a heavy, long-range bomber force. To achieve the desired result, the strategy was the bombing destruction of enemy civilian infrastructure and, thereby, the interruption of civilian life such that normal existence was no longer possible and, as a result, morale be irreparably damaged. The British Government, fired-up by the turmoil and panic that had been caused to the British civilian population from limited Zeppelin and Gotha raids, had concluded by extrapolation that a massive and sustained aerial bombing offensive might thoroughly destroy the national will of an enemy nation to resist. By the end of the 1920s, this had become the 'Trenchard doctrine' and it purported that heavy bombing alone could win a war if the Royal Air Force committed to it, in great enough aircraft numbers and high bombing intensity. It was to dominate Royal Air Force strategy through the 1930s and into World War II, perhaps best characterized under "Bomber Harris's" leadership[43].

The great shame was that, despite the adoption of strategic bombing as the raison d'être of Royal Air Force operations during Trenchard's tenure as Chief of the Air Staff, lessons such as the need for effective navigation,

---

[42] After the Armistice, British Survey Teams studied effectiveness of aerial bombardment. Little physical evidence of bomb damage was found and, indeed, there was no evidence to confirm that German aerial home defense had been strengthened in response to Independent Force operations. Defenders of strategic bombing turned to the argument that it remained a success because of the dire effect on German morale. Of course, this was impossible to prove one way or the other except for the anecdotal evidence of how the population of Britain had responded to the Zeppelin raids on Great Yarmouth, London and Hull. Proven or not, 'morale' was placed dead-center of Royal Air Force strategy to strike at the 'Achilles Heel' or bête noire enemy ability and will to fight on.

[43] Sir Arthur Travers Harris, (13 April, 1892 – 5 April, 1984), was known as "Bomber" Harris was Air Officer Commanding-in-Chief RAF Bomber Command during the WW II strategic bombing campaign against Nazi Germany. In 1942, the War Cabinet decided to undertake area bombing of German cities (Area Bombing Directive (General Directive No.5 (S.46368/111. D.C.A.S) dated 14 February, 1942) in order to dislocate the German industrial workforce effectiveness and degrade the morale of the German populace through bombing German cities and their civilian inhabitants. Harris was given the task of implementing the policy. Devastating attacks were conducted including the infamous raid on Dresden.

132

adverse weather capability, target identification, bombing accuracy and ability to deal with counter air defenses were not satisfactorily addressed. Trenchard had cause to recognize these deficiencies but was either intellectually not capable of discerning their importance or was so thoroughly exhausted merely fending off threats to an independent Royal Air Force that were not addressed until the later 1930s. The need for fighter escorts had been exhaustively demonstrated by the Independent Force DH-4/9/9A raids, so it is somewhat incomprehensible that nothing was done to place this at the centre of technical developments. The myopic persistence of the Royal Air Force with strategic area bombing doctrine continued through the 1920s, 30s and into the time of WW II (however, by the end of World War II, the Royal Air Force aircraft could drop bombs from 15,000 feet and strike within 75 feet with consistency – more precisely if bombing from a lower level). Undoubtedly, between-wars provision of inadequate funding had significant impact on the ability of the R.A.F. to innovate and develop new technologies, however, even more so, it seems to be clear that it was both Trenchard's presence and later his legacy that deterred new thinking on the development of disruptive military aerial warfare ideas. It is notable that the US Army, during this same period experimented and endeavored to develop 'precision bombing'. It is hard to escape the conclusion that the massive casualties sustained by Royal Air Force Bomber Command in WW II are part of Trenchard's legacy, reprising as they do the losses of his Independent Force. Enjoying the fullest command autonomy, R.A.F. attritional bombing strategy was accepted under his authority, and, because of this, his legacy must be to accept primary responsibility for the losses.

Trenchard's 1 January, 1919 memorandum to Weir is his effort to explain and justify his leadership decisions in command of the Independent Force, to anticipate and forestall immediate attacks from his nemesis, Sykes, and others and to provide a record for posterity. Sykes quickly fell afoul of Churchill because his proposals for the post-war Royal Air Force rebuilding plans were out of synch with the paucity of available defence funding and he was ousted in favor of Trenchard's return as Chief of the Air Staff on 31 March, 1919. There is no doubt that he possessed personal leadership qualities and, as his record as a young officer proves, he had qualities of resolution and bravery; the last of these showing again when he put down the '1919 Southampton Docks mutiny'. However, he was additionally self-absorbed, insubordinate, disobliging, pompous, coquettish, uncooperative, unscientific and apparently not evidently intellectually curious. In the case of the last, he did not find innovative ways, either technical or tactical to counter the horrendous attrition to his Independent Force aerial assets and he appeared to be content to continue bludgeoning away, with losses mounting until the lack of aircraft or aircrews stopped him – as misattributed to Albert Einstein, "insanity is doing the same thing over and over again and expecting different results" except, when loss of lives is involved, matters are entirely a more serious affair[44]. Similarly, after the war, despite being on the cusp of technical revolutions in most every branch of science and advanced thinking, he was slow to stimulate new operational approaches and advance aerial technology and, while the Royal Air Force survived, there were deep flaws in its cultural and warfighting effectiveness.

It is only right to finish this account of the Independent Force by reflecting on the airmen who served in it. It has been included as an appendix to the family story of a relation who died in combat 100 years ago to provide context to the loss. So far removed, the loss of great "Uncle Garrie" is not attended by hurt that would undoubtedly have been felt by those other relations contemporaneously who were close to him in 1918. However, research into the records that still exist, show that he did his duty and whether he was plain brave or made reckless by the risks that he faced as a nineteen year old, his record of low-level bombing was thoroughly remarkable and commentated on at the time by his Squadron Commanding Officer. The records of the commanders, notably the Air Minister, the Chief of the Air Staff and, in particular, the Chief of the Independent Force, Major-General Hugh Trenchard, are in this writer's view, less impressive. If the reader believes that this treatise has been too harsh on Trenchard, whose post-war career was stellar as he earned the epithet, "Father of the Royal Air Force", I can suggest only that the reader look back to source on how Trenchard conducted himself with his superiors, his peers and his subordinate squadron aircrews. Is it possible that such men as these occupied such high office?

For Trenchard to have sent young men into harm's way on missions and, on the evening of the Armistice in his personal diary, with a flourish he dismissed as a thorough "waste of effort and personnel" seems to be beyond belief. Winston Churchill on Neville Chamberlain's appeasements supposedly wrote, "Poor Neville will come badly out of history. I know, I

---

[44] The massive R.F.C. losses of "Bloody April" 1917 were due to fielding inferior technology, tactics and training and, faced with a similar scale of loss by the Independent Force in late 1918, Trenchard might have had reasonable cause to have a sense of déjà vu and, forewarned, a lesson learned, a better strategy than acceptance of attrition as a solution to allow continued raiding.

will write that history". Well, Hugh Trenchard is actually condemned by his own words and it would be unwise not to recognize this when lauding his paternity of the Royal Air Force, one hundred years after establishment; if, that is, we are to properly honour men such as Buck and Fowler in 215 Squadron and the many others that served and fell.

In his account to Weir, he paid tribute to his squadrons in the Independent Force. Trenchard recognized the courage of his pilots and observers and noted that his aircrews continued to operate despite cases in which losses amounted to most of the aircraft launched on a particular raid. World War I, with its aerial combat and other technical innovations, was certainly a first for truly modern warfare but many of its leaders, as mooted, such as Trenchard, appeared rooted in an extension of Victorian era and still embracing a culture that sacrifice on the battlefield could be passed off as glorious enterprise. Trenchard writes in stentorian terms of the "character of British pilots" that, "whatever their casualties were, if they could help shorten the war by one day and thus save many casualties to the Army on the ground they (believed they) were only doing their duty" and that he "never saw, even when our losses were heaviest, any wavering in their determination" to complete their missions. By suggesting it was the mission of the Independent Force to protect the Army gives the lie to the notion that he was employing the Independent Force squadrons as he had been ordered by the Air Ministry. He was instructed to strike strategic targets and engagement with tactical targets implies misappropriation of squadrons and unnecessary losses. "Glorious" warfare has no place in modern conflict and this was clearly understood by the young men in his aircrews even though they were obliged to obey the last order given. Maj W. R. Read, 216 Squadron noted the need to weigh the value of friendly losses against the amount of damage done to the enemy. 2nd Lieutenant Roy Shillinglaw, 100 Squadron, highlighted the profligacy of throwing aircrew indiscriminately into the fight and Major Nicholl, 110 Squadron, drew attention to the danger of using aircraft beyond their capability and, thereby, unnecessarily endangering aircraft. 2nd Lieutenant Goodfellow, 215 Squadron shared a similar experience to Shillinglaw and his recollections are included at Appendix R. Trenchard's unauthorized and profligate use of the Independent Force which resulted in great aircraft and personnel losses should not, must not, be covered by the blind that the aircrew were heroically keen and ready to make the greatest sacrifice. That is just not right. They were required to do their duty, irrespective of poor leadership.

One hundred years on and certainly we feel pride for the courage and commitment shown by British airmen such as pilot 2nd Lieutenant A.C.G. (Garrie) Fowler; and this is quite independent of whether his loss was necessary or not on the night 20/21 September, when he was brought down. His bravery and that of his companions, observer 2nd Lieutenant Clement Clough Eaves and gunlayer/observer 2nd Lieutenant John Shannon Ferguson bear witness to those peculiar and admirable human qualities that are sometimes found in men and women facing fearful odds whose outcome can be all too readily calculated. As for the architects and leaders of the Independent Force operations, men whose many statues and portraits reprove attempts to question their memory, well, the writer leaves it to an implacable and contemporary enemy to comment - General Erich Ludendorff[45] was reputed to have said:

"The English Generals are wanting in strategy. We should have no chance if they possessed as much science as their officers and men had of courage and bravery. They are lions led by donkeys."

---

[45] German general and the victor of the World War I Battles of Liège and Tannenberg and, from August 1916, he served as Quartermaster General, essentially, the leader of the German war efforts.

Appendix L

No. 215 Squadron Personnel

Limited information was available for NCOs, other ranks, maintainers and other squadron personnel

List limited to information accessed to date
Missions listed, where known, that relate to 2/Lt ACG Fowler

Name	Connection with Fowler	Fowler role in mission	Date	Mission and other information – Crew/Aircraft
Flt Sergt JB Abott	-	-	~1918	Awarded MSM in Jan 1919
2/Lt E Anderson	-	-	26 Sep 18	Propeller shot away and engine failure D4568
Flt Cdr JR Allen	-	-	-	Flew in HP O/100 1462
2/Lt JP Armitage	Friend Wrote condolence letter to family	-	6 Aug 18 11 Aug 18 22 Aug 18 13 Sep 18 14 Sep 18 20 Sep 18	Gunlayer with Capt. Williams D9865 Gunlayer with Capt. Williams D9865 Observer with Lt Lorimer D9863 Observer with Lt Kestell D9685 Observer with Lt Kestell C4734 Observer with Lt Kestell C9424
Attwood	-	-	15 Sep 18	Noted train movements on mission report
Lt John B Baldie	Killed in action	-	6 Nov 18	Born Largs ~1897 buried in Charmes Military Cemetery, Essegney, France.
2/Lt A K Barter	Fellow crew member	Gunlayer	6 Aug 18	Flew as observer with Buck pilot ,ACG as gunlayer Sprange as passenger Rly Annexe between Blanche Maison and Douai D9680
		Passenger	9 Aug 18	Flew as observer with Buck pilot, Preedy as gunlayer ACG as passenger Cambrai D9683
		Gunlayer	10 Aug 18	Flew as observer with Buck pilot, ACG as gunlayer Cambrai Gare Annexe D9693
		Gunlayer	12 Aug 18	Flew as observer with Buck pilot, ACG as gunlayer D9693
		Gunlayer	13 Aug 18	Flew as observer with Buck pilot, ACG as gunlayer Cambrai Gare Annexe D9693
		-	22 Aug 18	Flew as observer with Buck pilot, Lt Jones as gunlayer D9693

Name	Connection with Fowler	Fowler role in mission	Date	Mission and other information – Crew/Aircraft
		-	30 Aug 18 5 Sep 18	Flew as observer with Williams as pilot, Wadey gunlayer and Lacy as passenger Awarded DFC
Capt P Bewsher	-	-	-	Flew in HP O/100 1462
2/Lt N J Boon	-	-	20 Sep 18	Flew as gunlayer with Pilot Kestell C9424
2/Lt WH Brinkworth	-	-	-	Flew on HP O/400 D4567
AM A Brown	-	-	24 Jul 18	Flew as gunlayer with King to Armentières Rail Center in D9865
E F Brown	-	-	-	DFC citation
A G/L Browning	-	-	22 Aug 18 6,10,11Aug	Flew as gunlayer with Lieut J Lorimer as pilot and Armitage C9683 Flew as gunlayer with Darnton as pilot D9684
Lt RH Bruce	-	-	22 Oct 18	Flew with Lorimer as pilot and Thompson to Kaiserlautern C9743
Capt GS Buck MC DFC	Flew with ACG	Gunlayer Passenger Gunlayer Gunlayer Gunlayer -	6 Aug 18 9 Aug 18 10 Aug 18 12 Aug 18 13 Aug 18 22 Aug 18	Flew as pilot with Barter, ACG gunlyer, Sprague passenger Douai D9680 Flew as pilot with Barter, Preedy and ACG passenger Cambrai D9863 Flew as pilot with Barter and ACG gunlayer Cambrai D9863 Flew as pilot with Barter and ACG gunlayer D9863 Flew as pilot with Barter and ACG gunlayer Cambrai D9863 Flew as pilot with Barter and Jones D9863
J F Buckle	-	-	20 Sep 18	Flew 20/21 Sept, 18
Lt Cadwell	-	-	7 Mar 18	Mentioned in Lt Dickson's recommendation for award letter
2/Lt F Caton	-	-	30 Aug 18	Flew as passenger and shot in lung with pilot Purvis, observer Crombie, gunlayer Wade and 2nd passenger Yelverton in C9668 Boulay

Name	Connection with Fowler	Fowler role in mission	Date	Mission and other information – Crew/Aircraft
2/Lt WJN Chalklin	Flew with ACG	Pilot	2 Sep 18	ACG pilot, Chalklin gunlayer to Buhl D4568
		Pilot	3 Sep 18	ACG pilot, Chalklin gunlayer to Morhange D4568 Flew in HP O/400 C9683
Sergt Cherry	-	-	6 Aug 19	Flew as gunlayer with Roche as pilot and Millar D4566
		-	10 Aug 18	Flew as gunlayer with Roche as pilot and Millar D4566
		-	11 Aug 18	Flew as gunlayer with Roche as pilot and Millar D4566
		-	22 Aug 18	Flew as observer with Wilson as pilot and Mitchell D9664
Flt Sergt CG Coughtrey	-	-	Jan 1919	Mentioned in dispatches
Lt WE Crombie	-	-	6 Aug 18	Flew as observer with Purvis as pilot, Wade and Preedy passenger C9668
		-	10 Aug 18	Flew as observer with Purvis as pilot & Wade C9668
		-	11 Aug 18	Flew as observer with Purvis as pilot & Wade C9668
		-	22 Aug 18	Flew as observer with Purvis as pilot & Towill C9668
Sergt RE Culshaw	-	-	-	Flew HP O/400 C9720
2/Lt WR Dallas	-	-	20 Sep 18	Flew as gunlayer with Darnton as pilot
Capt RE Darnton	-	-	6 Aug 18	Flew as pilot with Jones and Browning, D9684
			10 Aug 18	Flew as pilot with Jones and Browning, D9684
			11 Aug 18	Flew as pilot with Jones and Browning, D9684
			22 Aug 18	Flew as pilot with Watters and Wadey D9685
			20 Sep 18	Flew as pilot with Murphy and Foulsham C9734
2/Lt H Davies	Flew with ACG	Pilot	2 Sep 18	Flew with ACG as pilot as passenger Buhl D4568
		Pilot	3 Sep 18	Flew with ACG as pilot as passenger Morhange D4568

Name	Connection with Fowler	Fowler role in mission	Date	Mission and other information – Crew/Aircraft
				Flew in HP O/400 C9673
Flt Lt E Dickson DSC	-	-	7 Mar 18	Letter noting act of exceptional bravery
Lt HR Dodd	Flew with ACG	Pilot - -	15 Sep 18 16 Sep 18 17 Sep 18	Flew with ACG as pilot as gunlayer Buhl D4568 Flew as pilot with Jeffkins and Fairhurst Frescaty C9658 Flew as pilot with Jeffkins and Fairhurst C9658 Dodd died other crew PoW
2/Lt RT Down	-	-	16 Sep 18	Flew with Lacy as pilot and Yelverton Mannheim D9864
2/Lt J Durie	-	-	26 Sep 18	Propeller shot away and engine failure D4568
2/Lt CC Eaves	Flew, and died, with ACG	Pilot	20 Sep 18	Flew as observer with ACG pilot and Ferguson gunlayer to Frescaty D9732 Died
2/Lt A Fairhurst	-	-	16 Sep 18 17 Sep 18	Flew as gunlayer with Dodd as pilot and Jeffkins to Frescaty C9658 Flew as gunlayer with Dodd as pilot and Jeffkins to Frescaty C9658 PoW (Dodd died)
2/Lt JS Ferguson	Flew, and died, with ACG	Pilot	20 Sep 18	Flew as gunlayer with ACG pilot and Eaves observer to Frescaty D9732 Died
Lt CC Fisher	Flew with ACG	Pilot	30 Aug 18 13 Aug 18 14Aug 18 16Sep 18	Flew as gunlayer with pilot ACG Boulay D4568 Flew as gunlayer with pilot ACG Cambrai D4568 Flew as gunlayer with pilot ACG D4568 Flew with Oakley and Locke to Cologne C9727
Sergt Foulsham	-	-	16Sep 18	Flew as gunlayer with Buckle as pilot. Returned twice with engine failure
2/Lt ACG		Passenger	6 Aug 18	Flew as passenger with Buck pilot to Rly

Name	Connection with Fowler	Fowler role in mission	Date	Mission and other information – Crew/Aircraft
Fowler				Annexe between Blanche Maison and Douai
		Passenger	9 Aug 18	Flew as passenger with Buck pilot to Cambrai but port engine failure
		Gunlayer	10 Aug 18	Flew as gunlayer with Buck pilot to Cambrai Gare Annexe
		Gunlayer	11 Aug 18	Flew as gunlayer with Lawson pilot to Cambrai (SE) Rly Annexe
		Gunlayer	12 Aug 18	Flew as gunlayer with Buck pilot
		Gunlayer	13 Aug 18	Flew as gunlayer with Buck pilot
		Pilot	14 Aug 18	Flew as pilot to Cambrai Gare Annexe
		Gunlayer	15 Aug 18	Flew as gunlayer with Lawson pilot to Cambrai Gare Annexe
		Pilot	22 Aug 18	Flew as pilot to Volkersweiller
		Pilot	23 Aug 18	Flew as pilot to Boulay
		Pilot	25 Aug 18	Flew as pilot to Boulay D4568
		Pilot	30 Aug 18	Flew as pilot to Boulay D4568
		Pilot	2 Sep 18	Flew as pilot to Buhl D4568
		Pilot	3 Sep 18	Flew as pilot to Morhange D4568
		Pilot	13 Sep 18	Flew as pilot to Courcelles D4568
		Pilot	14 Sep 18	Flew as pilot to Courcelles D4568
		Pilot	15 Sep 18	Flew as pilot to Buhl D4568
		Pilot	20 Sep 18	Flew as pilot to Frescaty, did not return C9732
2/Lt SJ Goodfellow	-	-	-	Flew in HP O/400 C9720
2/Lt C Guild	-	-	-	Flew in HP O/400 C9673
Lt HL Hammond	-	-	-	Flew in HP O/400 D4567
Sergt AG/L G Hare	-	-	6 Aug 18	Flew as gunlayer with Rees as pilot and Stott C9659
			10 Aug 18	Flew as gunlayer with Rees as pilot and Stott C9659
			11 Aug 18	Flew as gunlayer with Rees as pilot and Stott C9659
			22 Aug 18	Flew as gunlayer with Rees as pilot and Stott C9659
2/Lt AG Harrison	Flew with ACG	Pilot	30 Aug 18	Flew as passenger with ACG as pilot to Boulay D4568 Flew in HP O/400 C9673
Lt HE Hyde	-	-	-	Flew in D4566 with Monaghan and Mitchell

Name	Connection with Fowler	Fowler role in mission	Date	Mission and other information – Crew/Aircraft
2/Lt SG Jary	-	-	13 Sep 18	Flew with Kestell as pilot and Armitage to Metz D9658
			14 Sep 18	Flew with Kestell as pilot and Armitage to Ehrang C4734
			15 Sep 18	Flew with Kestell as pilot and Armitage to Buhl C4734
2/Lt AEC Jeffkins	-	-	16 Sep 18	Flew as observer with Dodd as pilot and Fairhurst to Frescaty C9568
			17 Sep 18	Flew as observer with Dodd as pilot and Fairhurst to Frescaty C9568 PoW, Dodd died
Lt H Jones	-	-	6 Aug 18	Flew as observer with Darnton as pilot and Browning D9864
		-	10 Aug 18	Flew as observer with Darnton as pilot and Browning D9864
		-	11 Aug 18	Flew as observer with Darnton as pilot and Browning D9864
		-	22 Aug 18	Flew as gunlayer with Buck as pilot and Barter D9683
2/Lt RE Kestell	-	-	10 Aug 18	To synchronize all watches by 8 pm
			11 Aug 18	Flew as pilot with Preedy and Wadey D4568
			13 Sep 18	Flew as pilot with Armitage and Jary to Metz D9658
			14 Sep 18	Flew as pilot with Armitage and Jary to Ehrang C4734
			20 Sep 18	Flew as pilot with Armitage and Boon C9424
Lt PDJ Kilmer	Adjutant for 83rd Wing CO	-	20 Sep 18	Signed order for Operation 20 September, 1918
2/Lt FE King	-	-	24 Jul 18	Flew and wounded as observer with Brown to Armentières Rail Center in D9865
2/Lt JB Lacy	-	-	16 Sep 18	Flew as pilot with Down and Yelverton to Mannheim D9864
Capt WB Lawson	Flew with ACG	-	10 Aug 18	Flew as pilot with Towill and Wadey C9658
		Gunlayer	11 Aug 18	Flew as pilot with Towill and ACG as gunlayer to Cambrai (SE) Railway Station C9658
2/Lt CJ	-	-	16 Sept 18	Flew with Fisher as pilot and Oakley to

Name	Connection with Fowler	Fowler role in mission	Date	Mission and other information – Crew/Aircraft
Locke				Cologne C9727
Lt J Lorimer	-	-	11 Aug 18 22 Aug 18 22 Oct 18	To synchronize all watches by 8 pm Flew as pilot with Armitage and Browning C9863 Flew as pilot with Bruce and Thompson to Kaiserlautern C9743
Lt McCormick	-	-	24 Sep 18	US Navy in 215 Squadron Died walking into propeller
Lt J Millar	-	-	6 Aug 18 11 Aug 18 22 Aug 18	Flew with Capt. JF Roche as pilot and Cherry D4566 Flew with Capt. JF Roche as pilot and Cherry D4566 Flew with Capt. JF Roche as pilot and Wade D4566
2/Lt GW Mitchell	-	-	6 Aug 18 10 Aug 18 11 Aug 18 18 Sep 18	Flew as observer with Wilson as pilot and Wadey D9864 Flew as observer with Wilson as pilot and Sprange D9864 Flew as observer with Wilson as pilot and Sprange D9864 Flew with pilot Monaghan to Cologne D4586
Lt HB Monaghan	-	-	18 Sep 18	Flew as pilot to Cologne with Mitchell D4586
Sergt WB Murphy	-	-	20 Sep 18 Nov 1918	Flew as Gunlayer with pilot Capt Darnton Awarded DFM
2/Lt RG Oakley	-	-	16 Sep 18	Flying with pilot Fisher and Locke to Cologne D9727
Sergt HT Phelby	-	-		Flew in HP O/400 D4567
2/Lt TV Preedy	Flew with ACG	- Passenger - - Pilot	6 Aug 18 9 Aug 18 10 Aug 18 11 Aug 18 14 Aug 18	Flew as passenger with Purvis as pilot, with Crombie and Wade C9668 Flew as gunlayer with Buck as pilot and Barter and ACG as passenger to Cambrai D 9653 Flew as observer with Williams as pilot, and Watters D9685 Flew as observer with Kestell as pilot and Wadey D4568 Flew as observer with pilot ACG to

143

Name	Connection with Fowler	Fowler role in mission	Date	Mission and other information – Crew/Aircraft
		Pilot	22 Aug 18	Cambrai Gare Annexe D4568 Flew as observer with pilot ACG to Volkersweiler D4568
		Pilot	23 Aug 18	Flew as observer with pilot ACG to Boulay D4568
		Pilot	25 Aug 18	Flew as observer with pilot ACG to Boulay D4568
		Pilot	30 Aug 18	Flew as observer with pilot ACG to Boulay D4568
		Pilot	2 Sep 18	Flew as observer with pilot ACG to Buhl Aerodrome D4568
		Pilot	13 Sep 18	Flew as observer with pilot ACG Courcelles D4568
		Pilot	14 Sep 18	Flew as observer with pilot ACG Courcelles D4568
		Pilot	15 Sep 18	Flew as observer with pilot ACG D4568
		-	20 Sep 18	Flew as observer with pilot Buckle Engine Failure
Lt MC Purvis	-	-	6 Aug 18	Flew as pilot, with Crombie and Wade and Preedy as passenger C9668
			10 Aug 18	Flew as pilot, with Crombie and Wade C9668
			11 Aug 18	Flew as pilot, with Crombie and Wade C9668
			22 Aug 18	Flew as pilot, with Crombie and Towill C9668 Flew in HP O/100 1462
FE Rees	-	-	6 Aug 18	Flew as pilot flew with Stott and Hare C9659
			10 Aug 18	Flew as pilot flew with Stott and Hare C9659
			11 Aug 18	Flew as pilot flew with Stott and Hare C9659
			22 Aug 18	Flew as pilot flew with Stott and Hare C9659
			23 Aug 16	Died
PVT HB Richards	-	-	27 Sep 18	Died
2/Lt JB Richardson	-	-		Flew in HP O/400 C9863
Capt JF Roche	-	-	6 Aug 18	Flew as pilot with Millar and Cherry D4566
			10 Aug 18	Flew as pilot with Millar and Cherry D4566

Name	Connection with Fowler	Fowler role in mission	Date	Mission and other information – Crew/Aircraft
			11 Aug 18	Flew as pilot with Millar and Cherry D4566
			22 Aug 18	Flew as pilot with Millar and Wade D4566
Sergt Sprange	Flew with ACG	Gunlayer	6 Aug 18	Flew as passenger with Buck as pilot, Barter, ACG as gunlayer to Railway Annexe between Blanche Maison and Douai D9680
		-	10 Aug 18	Flew as gunlayer with Wilson as pilot and Mitchell D9864
		-	11 Aug 18	Flew as gunlayer with Wilson as pilot and Mitchell D9864
		Pilot	14 Aug 18	Flew as gunlayer with ACG as pilot and Mitchell to Cambrai Gare Annexe D4568
		Pilot	22 Aug 18	Flew as gunlayer with ACG as pilot and Mitchell to Volkersweiler D4568
		Pilot	23 Aug 18	Flew as gunlayer with ACG as pilot and Mitchell to Boulay D4568
		Pilot	24 Aug 18	Flew as gunlayer with ACG as pilot and Mitchell to Boulay D4568
2/Lt J Stott	-	-	6 Aug 18	Flew as observer with Rees as pilot and Hare C9659
			10 Aug 18	Flew as observer with Rees as pilot and Hare C9659
			11 Aug 18	Flew as observer with Rees as pilot and Hare C9659
			22 Aug 18	Flew as observer with Rees as pilot and Hare C9659
2/Lt A Tapping	-	-	-	Flew in HP O/400 C9683
Lt CE Thompson	-	-	22 Oct 18	Flew with Lorimer as pilot and Bruce to Kaiserlautern C9743
Lt SE Towill	Flew with ACG	-	10 Aug 18	Flew as observer with Lawson as pilot with Wadey as gunlayer C9658
		Gunlayer	11 Aug 18	Flew as observer with Lawson as pilot with ACG as gunlayer to Cambrai (SE) Rly Station C9658
		Gunlayer	15 Aug 18	Flew as observer with Lawson as pilot with ACG as gunlayer to Cambrai Gare Annexe C9658
		-	22 Aug 18	Flew with Purvis as pilot and Crombie C9668
		-	16 Sep 18	To synchronize all watches by 8 pm
2/Lt JB	-	-	-	Flew in HP O/400 C9720

Name	Connection with Fowler	Fowler role in mission	Date	Mission and other information – Crew/Aircraft
Vickers				
Sergt Wade	-	-	6 Aug 18	Flew as gunlayer with Purvis as pilot, and Crombie and Preedy as passenger C9668
		-	10 Aug 18	Flew as gunlayer with Purvis as pilot, and Preedy C9668
		-	11 Aug 18	Flew as gunlayer with Purvis as pilot, and Crombie C9668
		-	22 Aug 18	Flew with Capt. JF Roche as pilot and Millar D4566
Sergt EW Wadey		-	6 Aug 18	Flew as observer with Wilson as pilot, and Mitchell D9664
		-	10 Aug 18	Flew as gunlayer with Lawson as pilot, and Towill as observer C9685
		-	11 Aug 18	Flew as gunlayer with Kestell as pilot and Preedy D4569
		-	22 Aug 18	Flew as gunlayer with Capt A – Williams pilot, with Watters D9685
		-	Oct 1918	Awarded DFM
2/Lt AH Watters	-	-	6 Aug 18	Flew as observer with Williams as pilot, and Armitage D9685
		-	10 Aug 18	Flew as observer with Williams as pilot, and Preedy D9685
		-	11 Aug 18	Flew as observer with Williams as pilot, and Armitage D9685
		-	22 Aug 18	Flew as observer with as Williams pilot and Wadey D9685
		-	30 Aug 18	Awarded DSM
Capt A Watts-Williams	-	-	6 Aug 18	Flew as pilot with Mitchell and Wadey D9664
		-	10 Aug 18	Flew as pilot, with Watters and Preedy D9685
		-	11 Aug 18	Flew as pilot, with Watters and Armitage D9685
		-	22 Aug 18	Flew as pilot, with Watters and Wadey D9685
		-	5 Sep 18	Awarded DSM
2/Lt GW Wilson	-	-	6 Aug 18	Flew as pilot with Mitchell and Wadey D9664
		-	10 Aug 18	Flew as pilot with Mitchell and Sprange D9664
		-	11 Aug 18	Flew as pilot with Mitchell and Sprange D9864
		-	22 Aug 18	Flew as pilot with Mitchell and Cherry D9664

Name	Connection with Fowler	Fowler role in mission	Date	Mission and other information – Crew/Aircraft
2/Lt CN Yelverton	-	-	16 Sept 18	Flew with pilot Lacy flying D9864 to Mannheim with Down

Appendix M

2nd Lieutenant A.C.G Fowler Newspaper Clippings and RAF Casualty Record Card

HITCHIN FLYING OFFICER,

OFFICIALLY REPORTED KILLED.

We regret to state that official news has been received of the death of a young Hitchin flying officer, 2nd-Lieut. A. C. G. Fowler, R.A.F., younger son of the late Mr. Alfred Fowler, of Hitchin.

Since he was reported missing after a had been entertained of his safety. The Prisoners of War Agency in Switzerland has received from Germany a notification of his death. The report states that Lieut. Fowler was brought down and killed on September 21, on the aerodrome of Fresksty, near Metz. His grave is in the military cemetery of Metz, marked so that it can be found by the family.

The gallant death of Lieut. Fowler will be regretted by many old school friends in the Hitchin district. An elder brother, Corpl. B. P. Fowler, is with the A.S.C. (M.T.) Mrs. Hubert Moss is a sister.

2ND-LIEUT, A. C. G. FOWLER MISSING,

"A BRAVE AVIATOR AND A GENTLEMAN."

We regret to learn that 2nd-Lieutenant A.C.G. Fowler, R.A.F., son of the late Mr. and Mrs. Alfred Fowler, of Hitchin, is missing.

Lieutenant J. P. Armitage, R.A.F., has written to Mrs. Bourne, a sister of 2nd-Lieutenant Fowler as follows:—"Your brother unfortunately was one of this squadron's missing on September 20. The A.C.G., as he was called by the boys in the mess, was one of the most popular chaps here, and although he did not come out with the original squadron, was looked upon by the few that are left, as part and parcel of that original crowd. I lived in the same hut as he, and, in consequence, was one of his greatest pals. As a pilot he was superb, and was among the best that it has ever been my pleasure as an observer, to fly with. Only the day previous we had the good news that the two of us would shortly be proceeding to England on a special job; now, unfortunately, this has happened, so that takes the spice off the thing as far as I am concerned. I hear that he had been recommended for a decoration, and know for a fact that he was mentioned in despatches a couple of times. He was a brave aviator and a gentleman."

Figure 34: Hertfordshire Gazette Reports 5 October, 1918

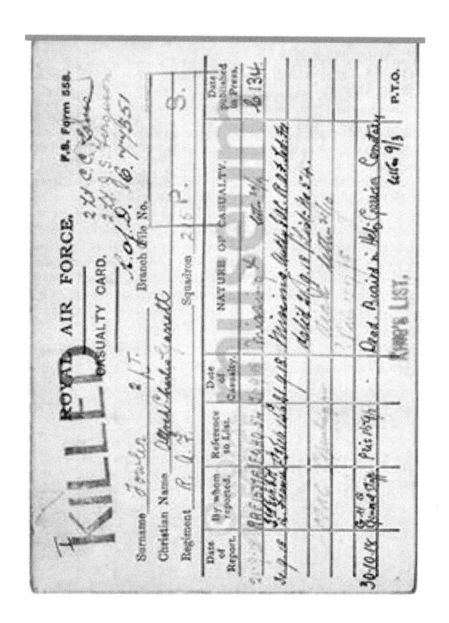

Figure 35: 2nd Lieutenant A.C.G. Fowler's Casualty Record Card (TNA Kew UK)

149

Appendix N

Frescaty Aerodrome Today

The German Frescaty Aerodrome later became a French Air Force Metz-Frescaty Air Base is located approximately 5 miles (8.0 km) south-southwest of Metz and around 174 miles (280 km) east of Paris.

After the defeat of France in the 1871 Franco-Prussian War, Metz and much of the Moselle were annexed by Germany as part of the Treaty of Frankfurt. Metz became a garrison town for the German Army. In 1909, the German Army developed an airship field to the SW of Metz including a Zeppelin hangar in the northern corner. During World War I, in addition Zeppelin operations, German combat aircraft stationed at Frescaty operated over the Western Front. Following the Armistice, France acquired the Alsace region and the airfield was taken over by the French Air Force, only to be lost again during World War II. As a German military airfield, it was extensively bombed by Allied aircraft and buildings such as the Zeppelin hangar, the Casino de Frescaty and other structures were totally destroyed. Post World War II, France again took possession, and the airfield was operated as an active military base until 2017 when it was placed on reserve status.

In the following maps (figures 36, 37 and 38), positions of the World War I contemporary structure are shown.

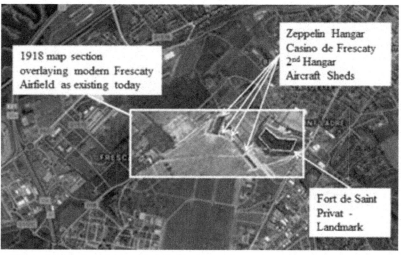

Figure 36: Modern Frescaty Airfield with a section overlay of a 1918 overhead reconnaissance photograph (Google Maps © 2018)

150

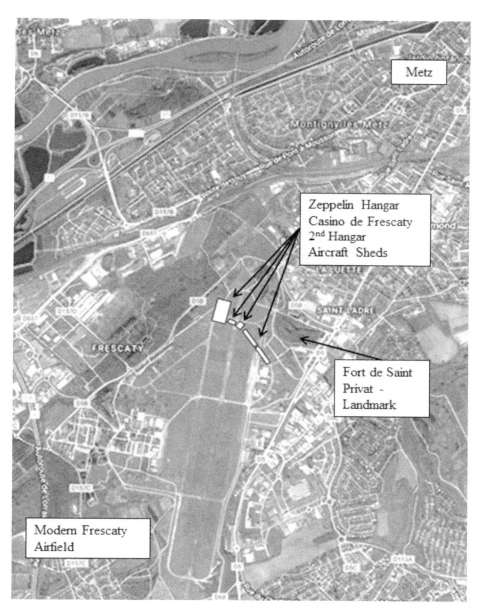

Figure 37: Position of principal World War I structure overlaying modern Frescaty airfield
(Google Maps © 2018)

151

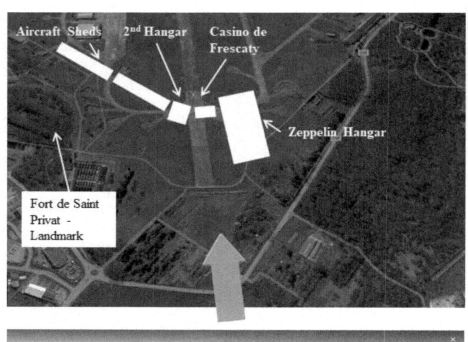

Frescaty Aerodrome From The North Looking South, South-West

Figure 38: Frescaty Aerodrome structure as it would have been located in September 1918
(Google Maps © 2018)

152

Appendix O

Handley Page 0/400 C9732 Aircrew: 20 September, 1918

Written by Anne Gillatt for Imperial War Museum (IWM) Lives of the First World War

2nd Lieutenant Alfred Charles Garrett Fowler: 17 June, 1899 - 21st September 1918

Fowler was born on 17 June, 1899, the son of Alfred and Fanny Fowler of "The Lodge", Chiltern Road, Hitchin, Hertfordshire, UK. He was born in Hitchin Union Workhouse where his father was the Master and his mother, Matron. Younger brother to Constance, Bernard and Christabel Ann, and an elder step-sister Gertrude Jane Agnes. He attended Hitchin Grammar School from 1907 to 1913. On the death of his parents, he became a pupil of the East Anglian School, Bury-St-Edmunds. In1917 he was awarded the Science Special Prize and a distinction in Chemistry in the Cambridge Local Examinations and thereafter, he then attended the Polytechnic in Regent Street, London SW1, UK as an Electrical Engineering student. On 14 June,1917 Fowler joined RNVR Division Mersey No Z 3621 (height recorded as 6ft 2ins/chest-36 $^3/_4$ ins/eyes-blue). Rating as Able Seaman HMS Victory VI (Crystal Palace - used as training depot for the Royal Navy) between 24 July to 20 October, 1917 he trained as Wireless telegraphy, W/T operator. On 20 October, 1917 approved for discharge from RNVR with a view to obtaining a commission as a Probationary Flight Officer RNAS). He Joined RNAS at Greenwich as Temporary Probationary Flying Officer on 28 October, 1917. He transferred to Manston 3 December, 1917 for flying instruction and again, transferred to Cranwell 30 March, 1918. Machines flown - M/Farman, Avro and BE2C. On 1 April, 1918 the RNAS became the Royal Air Force. His rank changed to Probationary 2nd Lieutenant. Results of his Graduation Examination May 1918 - Flying ability 2nd class/Wireless Telegraphy 96.6% 1st class/Photography 96.6% 1st class. Appointed Temporary 2nd Lt 1 May, 1918. Cranwell recorded 55 hours 28 minutes flying time. Remarks on Graduation – "graduated/very good pilot and Officer/recommended for Handley Page machines/very reliable and shows good judgement/is very tall and heavy and most suitable for Handley Page bombers." He joined 215 Squadron following their re-equipping with O/400s (the Squadron returned from Couderkerque (near Dunkirk), France to Netheravon 25 April, 1918 to replace existing HP O/100 machines with HP O/400 machines). 215 Squadron moved to Andover 15 May, 1918 and returned to France on 4 July, 1918, basing at Alquines as part of the newly formed Independent Force. 215 Squadron moved again on 19 August, 1918 to a new base at Xaffévillers. 2nd/Lt Fowler's flying time to 11 July, 1918 was 80 hours and 35 minutes. By the time that he was shot down, he had conducted 14 bombing missions as pilot and aircraft captain. Additionally, during early August while qualifying to pilot operation missions, he flew on seven theatre familiarization raids, five of which were as gunlayer. By 20th September he had flown 21 missions in all, including raids on Fosperweiller, Boulay, Buhl and Morhange aerodromes. On 15th September, piloting his own H P D4568, he flew two sorties in one night from Xaffévillers. His Observer was 2nd Lt Thomas Victor Preedy (who accompanied him on a number of missions but not on 20 September, 1918) and Gunlayer 2nd Lt Hugh Reginald Dodd. The crew missing on the night of 20/21 September, 1918 (Frescaty Aerodrome raid) in aircraft C9732 was - pilot: 2nd Lt A.C.G. Fowler/Observer: 2nd Lt Clement Clough Eaves/Gunlayer: 2nd Lt John Shannon Ferguson. The aircraft C9732 was a new machine taken on charge by 215 Squadron on 17 September, 1918. The independent Force casualty returns for September 1918 show C9732 as shot down in flames near Metz and the crew buried in Metz Garrison Cemetery, although The War Graves Commission record no known grave. As such the name of 2nd Lt A.C.G. Fowler is carved on the Flying Services Memorial in the Arras Memorial to the Missing at Fauberg d'Amiens Cemetery, Arras, France, with his crew members. His name is also recorded on the Hitchin War Memorial in St Mary's Churchyard and on the Roll of Honour at Hitchin Grammar School.

2nd Lieutenant Clement Clough Eaves: 18th February 1894 - 21st September 1918

Eaves was born on 18 February, 1894 in Derby, UK. His parents were Elam Eaves and Amelia Clough. He had an older brother, Elam and two younger sisters, Ena Mary and Edna. The 1901 Census has the family living at 96, Chatham Street, Edgeley, Stockport. On the 2 April, 1911 Census he is listed as an apprentice engineer, and living at 3, Didsbury Road, Heaton Norris, Stockport. He attended Manchester Technical College. From 1909 to 1916 Clement Eaves was working as a diesel engine expert at Messrs. Mirralees, Buckerton, Day Ltd of Hazel Grove, Stockport. From 1916 to 1918 he was involved in aero engine inspection at Aeronautical Inspection Directorate, Manchester. Clement Clough Eaves signed his Short Term Army Attestation on 10 December, 1915 in Dunfermline. His rank was Private in the Army Reserve. His height is recorded as 5 feet 11½ inches. He was called to The

Colours and appointed to the Royal Flying Corps on 18 June, 1917. Transferred to Army Reserve Class "W" on 30 May, 1917 with rank of 2/AM (Air Mechanic 2nd Class). Re-firmed to The Colours from Class "W" Army Reserve 25 March, 1918. Rank 2/AM. Transferred to RAF 1st April 1918 under provisions Air Force (Constitution) Act 1917. Rank AM3 (Air Mechanic Class 3). On 9 April, he underwent aircrew selection and was assessed as being unsuitable for pilot training, but suitable as an observer. Clement Eaves undertook observer training at Blackdown, Surrey, through August. With flight training completed by 10 August he qualified as an observer on 23 August. 13 July, 1918 - from RD to 1SAG(H). 27 July, 1918 - from 1SAG(H) to 1SAG(R). 10 August, 1918 - from 1SAG(R) to 6 Brigade (47 Wing). 6 September, 1918 - discharged under Kings Regs for RAF on appointment to a temporary commission. 6 September, 1918 - granted a temporary commission as a 2nd Lt (Observer Officer). Entry in the London Gazette dated 10 September, 1918 refers. 8 September, 1918 - from 6 Brigade (51 Sqn.) to BEF. In September 1918 he is a 2nd Lt with 215 Squadron RAF at Xaffévillers, as a member of a three man crew flying Handley Page 0/400 heavy bombers. On the night of 20/21 September, 1918 his plane C9732 took off from Xaffévillers at 20:08 hours with six other Handley Page 0/400 aircraft on a mission to bomb targets at Frescaty. Two aircraft returned with bombs intact and four reached the objective. One aircraft C9732 was reported missing on the night of 20/21 September - the pilot was 2nd Lt Alfred Charles Garrett Fowler, the observer was 2nd Lt Clement Clough Eaves and the gunlayer[46] 2nd Lt John Shannon Ferguson. Aircraft C9732 was a new machine taken on charge by 215 Squadron on 17 September, 1918. The Independent Force casualty returns for September 1918 show C9732 as shot down in flames near Metz, and the crew buried in Metz Cemetery, although the War Grave Commission record no known grave. Therefore, the name of 2nd Lt Clement Clough Eaves is carved on the Arras Flying Services Memorial in the Arras Memorial to the Missing at Fauberg d'Amiens, France with his crew members. RIP.

2nd Lieutenant John Shannon Ferguson (Photograph from Hawick News & Border Chronicle 13 December, 1918 – see Page 19): 25th August 1894 - 21st September 1918

---

[46] As gunlayer, Ferguson manned the rear cockpit and the two upper and single lower machine guns. In the event of bomb 'hang-ups', he would have responsibility for freeing the bombs, if he could. He would also throw the 25 lb Cooper bombs on target. But, manning the upper machine guns requited some care, since, as warned by Lieutenant Monaghan in his flying recollections, crew new to the gunlayer position would be warned that the "upper two had no check point and it was possible to shoot the tail off."

Ferguson was born on 25 August, 1894 in Hawick, Roxburgh, Scotland. His parents were Thomas Ferguson and Mary Anne Shannon. Thomas was born in Hawick and Mary Anne in Wilton, Roxburgh. At the time of his parents' deaths (1933/1935), they were living at 170 Elm Street, Pittsfield, Massachusetts, USA. In the 1901 Census, John was registered as living with his family at 20, Gladstone Street, Hawick, Roxburgh. His siblings are recorded as William 22 (woollen power loom turner), Hugh 20 (apprentice joiner), Maggie 18 (wool hosiery machinist), Thomas 16 (apprentice grocer), Annie 11 (scholar), Andrew 6 (scholar), and Jane 4. His elder brother Andrew, Canadian Engineers, was killed in action in France on 27 March, 1918. John Shannon Ferguson moved to the USA at some stage, and possibly left Glasgow on the ship, Parisian, and arrived in Boston, Massachusetts on 23 May, 1912. His Army Service began on 17 August, 1915. His home address is recorded as 2, Trevelyn Terrace, Hawick. Next of Kin (mother) - Annie Ferguson, 276 East Street, Pittsfield, Massachusetts, USA. His civilian occupation was as a chauffeur. Joined Royal Flying Corps 17 August, 1915. Transferred 1/AM 11 September, 1915 (Air Mechanic Class 1). Appointed 2/AM 1 September, 1916 (Air Mechanic Class 2). Joined Royal Air Force (mechanic) 1 April, 1918. His Medical Examination Board and aircrew selection process on 10 May, 1918 records his assessment as being unsuitable for pilot training, but suitable as an observer. Height as 5 feet 6 $^3/_4$ ins. In September 1918, he was a 2nd Lt with 215 Squadron RAF based at Xaffévillers, as a crew member flying Handley Page 0/400 heavy bombers. On the night of 20/21 September, 1918 his plane C9732 took off from Xaffévillers at 20:08 hours with six other Handley Page 0/400 bombers to bomb targets at Frescaty. Two aircraft returned with bombs intact and four aircraft reached the objective. His aircraft C9732 was reported missing on the night of 20/21 September,1918. The pilot was 2nd Lt Alfred Charles Garrett Fowler and the observer was 2nd Lt Clement Clough Eaves. 2nd Lt John Shannon Ferguson was the gunlayer. Aircraft C9732 was a new machine taken on charge by 215 Squadron on 17 September, 1918. The Independent Force casualty returns show C9732 as shot down in flames near Metz and the crew buried in Metz Cemetery, although the War Graves Commission record no known grave. Therefore, the name of 2nd Lt John Shannon Ferguson is carved on the Flying Services Memorial in the Arras Memorial to the Missing at Fauberg d'Amiens, Arras, France, along with his crew members. An article in The Scotsman Newspaper of 5 October, 1918 reports "Observation Officer John Ferguson R F C (missing) is the son of Mr T Ferguson, Pittsfield, Mass, formally of Hawick. He enlisted in 1915, when he came from America for the purpose". Another report in The Hawick News and Border Chronicle of 13 December, 1918 headed "2nd Lieut J S Ferguson - Independent Force previously reported missing on 21st Sept, is now officially reported killed in action. He was 24 years of age, and the youngest son of Mr. and Mrs. T Ferguson, Pittsfield, Mass, and is the second son to have made the ultimate sacrifice. Another brother is at present in France. He has two married brothers residing in Hawick - William Ferguson, Buccleuch Street and Hugh Ferguson, Trevelyn Terrace".

Appendix P

No. 55 Squadron "In Formation" Song

No. 55 Squadron's song, 'In Formation', was based on the song, 'Widows Are Wonderful' that had won fame in wartime Britain as part of an extremely successful musical called *Yes, Uncle!* that premiered at London's Prince of Wales Theatre in December 1917. The lyrics were written by Clifford Grey and the music by Nat D. Ayer (for those having interest, it was released on Columbia Records, number 2880 and is rendered today on *YouTube*). Wags in 55 Squadron wrote new words and probably sang it raucously as they quaffed a few beers to relax outside operations. The song praises the D.H.4 and its Rolls-Royce engine (more powerful than the D.H.9 engine) and asserts the value of formation flying – defence measure against enemy fighter attacks. Lastly, it digs at No. 99 Squadron who flew the inferior D.H.9 and invites them to match their efforts.

On your first formation
In a D.H.4.
You'll have a sensation
You've had before

You may think you're "Split-ace"
And all that sort of rot;
But try some close formation
And you'll learn a lot.

Our bus is wonderful, you must
Admit that's true,
My lad, I'm telling you
And the Rolls-Royce in her, too.

Our bus is marvelous, of course,
It has to be.
It's a D.H.4. I need say no more, but-Thumbs up,
That's all!

Our bus is dangerous, the Huns
Know us quite well, Mannheim
Coblenz, Mainz, and all the rest.

To the Rhine when it's fine
Come along with us 99
And bomb away every day.
As we've done all this year.

Appendix Q

<u>Lieutenant Hugh B. Monaghan, RAF</u>

Hugh Monaghan was a Canadian who enlisted in the army in 1915, subsequently transferred to the R.F.C. in 1917 and, after qualification as a pilot, joined No. 216 Squadron in Autreville, France in 1918. Monaghan later recounted that he thought that the 216 personnel, who were mostly former R.N.A.S., were perhaps a little haughty and his relaxed colonial ways and buff R.F.C uniform were not received empathetically. He also felt that he had to exert himself a little too hard to be included in familiarity missions to achieve operational qualification to pilot his own aircraft. Having completed three such missions, he was brought down and hospitalized by influenza.

After recovering, he was transferred to 215 Squadron which proved to be a much happier fit, there being several Canadian aircrew on squadron strength already. He was made operationally qualified immediately and he took on Handley Page O/400 D4566. His operational career was short and completed eight operations only, before his attack on Cologne on the night of 16/17 September. Accompanied by Lieutenant G.W. Mitchell (observer) and Lieutenant H.E. Hyde (gunlayer), after an explosion that destroyed the port engine at 5,000 feet over enemy territory, he somehow brought the aircraft down, apparently without aileron control, to pile up luckily in telegraph lines that cushioned the impact with the ground.

Figure 39: Lieutenant High B. Monaghan R.F.C/R.A.F

Monaghan's No. 100 Squadron friend, 2/Lieutenant Roy Shillinglaw with whom he met up with several times between 1970 and his death on 10 April 1974, wrote a tribute to him and it is included below.

"I first met Hugh Monaghan in 1918 at Xaffévillers aerodrome which was one of the operational aerodromes of the Independent Force in Lorraine, France in which we both had the privilege of serving. While Hugh was with 215 Squadron, I was in No. 100 Squadron and our respective aeroplanes were usually alongside each other waiting for take-off.

I remember very well the night Hugh failed to return and was posted missing. It was a beautiful moonlight night but an increasing adverse wind which would only allow a ground speed of about 35 to 40 miles per hour for the long plod home on a mission of about six to seven hours duration. The aeroplanes of those days were made entirely of wood strongly braced and covered with linen fabric and were very robust. It was as well they were so, for no parachutes were used and if one was disabled by enemy fire which at times was very intense the plane had to be brought down, and if possible, home, not only to save the machine but also the lives of the pilot and his crew.

This happened to Hugh at a height of 6,000 feet when he was loaded with nearly a ton of bombs and there is no doubt it was due to his flying skill that he brought the crippled machine down in a near vertical sideslip and hit a large bunch of telegraph wires which saved the lives of his two colleagues and himself.

Fifty-four years later, Hugh and I made a nostalgic trip visiting our two operational aerodromes at Ochey and Xaffévillers and a look at some of our old targets. Eventually, we arrived at Cochem, 20 miles southwest of Coblenz in the Moselle Valley where Hugh was shot down. We looked at the wood in which he hid for a couple of days until the police dogs ferreted him out and he had to surrender to become a prisoner of war.

At Cochem the valley is only a quarter of a mile wide or so and flanked by near vertical mountains on both sides and it is a miracle Hugh's aeroplane slipped into that particular spot in the middle of the night. It is with great pride I retain the memory of Hugh and of my friendship with him. He was a man of the utmost integrity and courage. In those days we had a toast, "Happy Landings". I am sure Hugh has landed safely again.

Roy Shillinglaw

Ex-Observer 100 Squadron

Independent Air Force

Castletown, Isle of Man"

160

Appendix R

2nd Lieutenant Sampson J. Goodfellow, RAF

Winston Churchill had the wit to understand that the writers of events, whether they are retired British Prime Ministers, Egyptian Pharaohs or simply bystanders, are witnesses who determine whether a personage comes out well or like "poor Neville (Chamberlin)", they "come badly out of history." However, there is another problem, which is that the vast majority of historical events do not have the benefit of someone on hand to witness them or to make written record for posterity. Furthermore, paper is a flimsy material and even those written works that are made, are often lost, decay with time, are not recognized as important or are destroyed. Sometimes this is on a grand scale like the burnings of the ancient Library of Alexandria and other times, because they remain hidden - unpretentious as undisclosed memoirs by family members in written musings – they stay lost in private collections modestly eschewing any pretention to importance. Occasionally, such material emerges to provide a new perspective and to require a revision of history or at the very least, filling in some of the blanks. Such may be the case with Edward Willett who found the memoirs of his wife's grandfather, 2nd Lieutenant Sampson J. Goodfellow, a Canadian No. 215 Squadron Handley Page O/400 Observer, who flew missions as part of the Independent Force during the final two months of World War I. Willett published these memoirs in an on-line Blog and provides a useful contemporary insight to the leadership and history of the Independent Force.

Goodfellow appears to have been operational during the month October 1918 and probably joined 215 Squadron in late September. Writing in later years, he said that, although he no longer possessed his flying log, he recalled from memory that he had raided Saarbrücken, Thionville, Karlsruhe, Strasbourg, and Ecouviez Rail Junction. In an aside to the extremely high losses that were sustained by Trenchard's Command, he observed that "when you were with the Independent Air Force you only made 5 or 6 trips and that was all I made."

In October 1918, winter weather caused major disruption to bombing raids in the Independent Force theatre of operations. In early September, there had been spells of poor weather that disrupted aerial efforts in support of the St. Mihiel offensive. However, in October, meteorologically induced "chill fogs" descended from the Vosges Mountains and reduced flying visibility such that the Handley Page squadrons could barely find their way back to home aerodromes, let alone find the target. On sixteen days in the month of October, no attacks on industrial centres were achieved and the tonnage of bombs dropped during the month fell to 98 tons compared with the 179 tons dropped in September. Nevertheless, the Handley Page squadrons accrued 1,828 flying hours in October – some 223 hours more than in September indicating that aircraft were launching on raids but were unable to reach their target. Sometimes they returned with their bomb loads intact. It seems to be clear that the Handley Page squadrons were making great efforts, however, their aircraft, equipment and training fell well short of what was required to achieve successful bombing missions in what would be considered in modern times, instrument-rated weather conditions.

By mid-October, Trenchard was apparently becoming increasingly frustrated with the failure of his Independent Force aircrews to fulfill his planned aggressive bombing campaign. Shortly after taking command of the Independent Force he had admonished Squadron Commanders to be more aggressive about flying in adverse weather and to have their crews fly two or three missions in a single night. He had also given pep talks to aircrew gathered to hear him, (as recounted, for example, by 2nd Lieutenant Roy Shillinglaw, No. 100 Squadron) setting the tone regarding his priorities for his aircrews' preservation. One had only to look at the squadron's massive loss rates to confirm that there was no

Figure 40: 2nd Lieutenant Sampson J. Goodfellow, RAF
(Courtesy Edward Willett)

misunderstanding on this matter. He told them quite clearly that they were expendable.

It appears that Trenchard also vented this frustration with a series of later visits to his squadrons in October 1918 with the objective to vim up their performance.

Goodfellow says that Trenchard visited all the nine squadrons and his meeting with the 215 aircrew was at 23:00 (believed to be 29 October, 1918) and coincident with when they were about to fly. He says that Trenchard was accompanied by the Duke of York[47] (future King George VI). Whether by design or embarrassment, when Trenchard began his address, the Duke of York retreated to stand in a corner and apparently, said nothing. Goodfellow wrote that Trenchard gave 215 Squadron aircrew 'hell' and, as he warmed to his brief, "he swore at us, called us liars, and said we dropped the bombs in fields near our objective and came back with stories that were not true." Trenchard went on to say, "Every plane is going over tonight from (the) five Handley Page Squadrons…and don't any of you come back before going to your objective" and "…the Handley Page only costs 50,000 pounds, so don't worry; we have lots of Planes and lots of flyers to take your place." Needless to say, Goodfellow was not much impressed and in a side commentary, he says plainly that the claimed existence of "lots of (replacement) aircraft and flyers," was an untruthful statement. Still, he was evidently shaken by the verbal barrage and happening to be stood directly in front of Trenchard during the rant, Goodfellow observes, "…when he called us liars, I thought he meant me."

With Trenchard's admonition resonating still in his mind, Goodfellow was scheduled to attack Ecouvez Rail Junction that night. Flying in Handley Page C9720, with pilot 2nd Lieutenant J.B. Vickers and gunlayer Sergeant R.E. Culshaw, Goodfellow launched to attack Ecouvez on the evening of 29/30 October, 1918. Navigating using the lighthouses as directional way-points, C9720 found the second lighthouse but the mist then rolled in and the third lighthouse was elusive and was found only after having to backtrack twice.

Goodfellow says that Vickers suggested turning back because of the mist, which was now "good and thick," but he said to the pilot, "No chance!" Vickers remonstrated, "I don't know where we are ", to which he responded, "Neither do I, for I can't see any landmarks, but keep going on them degrees (flying course) and then I will get a bearing." A short while later, Goodfellow saw the Moselle River and the glow of a steel mill which gave him a sense of their situation. Vickers, presumably still not convinced that they could find Ecouvez, remained keen to turn back for home but the 'Colonial' Goodfellow, apparently still bruised by Trenchard's words,

---

[47] Albert, Duke of York and future King George VI was posted to serve on Major General Trenchard's Independent Force staff headquarters in Nancy, France. He arrived on 23 October and remained in post for the closing weeks of the war.

exclaimed, "No. No English Devil is going to call me a liar or say I am a coward, so keep going." Finding a railroad, matching his planned route, Goodfellow was able to navigate C9720 to the Ecouvez Rail Junction and they dropped their bombs. They then strafed the target, increasing altitude to rise above return tracer fire only to be hit by anti-aircraft fire and, with both engines knocked-out and the lower starboard wing and undercarriage shot away, C9720 likely spun into the ground. Goodfellow says that he thought to himself in that moment, "Good-bye, they have got you this time" and he observed that ". . . it is a peculiar thing: you are not afraid to die. You have been so well trained it does not bother you." The aircraft piled in to the ground but, serendipitously, a stand of trees broke their fall and, other than Vickers suffering a broken ankle, they reported no more than, perhaps, cuts and bruises. However, they had crashed in enemy territory and shortly afterwards, German soldiers carrying rifles, bayonets fixed, arrived to prod them into captivity as prisoners of war. Goodfellow's aerial war was over...and he was still alive!

Abbreviations

1/AM	Air Mechanic First Class
2/AM	Air Mechanic Second Class
AA	Anti-aircraft Artillery
AEF	American Expeditionary Force
AM	Air Mechanic
ASC(M/T)	Army Service Corps (Motor Transport)
BEF	British Expeditionary Force
BE.2c	Royal Aircraft Factory "Bleriot Experimental" 2c
BHP	Beardmore-Halford-Pullinger engine
Btn	Battalion
CAS	Chief of Air Staff
CO	Commanding Officer
CPO	Chief Petty Officer
CWGC	Commonwealth War Graves Commission
DFC	Distinguished Flying Cross
DFM	Distinguished Flying Medal
DFO	Directorate of Flying Operations
DH	DH 4, DH 9/A De Havilland aircraft
DSC	Distinguished Service Cross
EA	Enemy Aircraft
EF	Engine Failure
ET	Engine Trouble
F.E.2b	Royal Aircraft Factory et al "Farman Experimental" 2b, called the "Fee"
FGO	Flaming Green Onions

Flak	Flugzeugabwehrkanone: German meaning aircraft-defense cannon
GAvA	Guild of Aviation Artists
GOC	General Officer Commanding
GPS	Global Positioning Satellite
HE	High Explosive
HP	Handley Page HP O/100, HP O/400 aircraft
h.p.	Horse power (or HP)
HQ	Headquarters
IF	Independent Force
IWM	Imperial War Museum
JSCSC	Joint Services Command and Staff College
KIA	Killed in Action
MC	Military Cross
m/c	Machines (refers to aircraft)
M-Flack	Maschinenkanone Flak: German machine gun
MG	Machine Gun
MSM	Meritorious Service Medal
NCO	Non-commissioned Officer
PoW	Prisoner of War
PVT	Private
RAF	Royal Air Force
Regt	Regiment
Res	Reserve
RFC	Royal Flying Corps
RL 112 lb	Royal Laboratory 112 lb (bomb)
RN	Royal Navy

RNAS	Royal Naval Air Service
RNVR	Royal Naval Voluntary Reserves
RPM	Revolutions per Minute
SAA	Small Arms Ammunition
SAG	School of Aerial Gunnery
SIO	Squadron Intelligence Officer
SO	Signalling Onions (=FGO Flaming Green Onions)
Sqdn	Squadron
TNT	Trinitrotoluene
USN	United States Navy
VC	Victoria Cross

Bibliography

1. The National Archives of the U.K. AIR 1/1946/204/249/1 Record book. 1918 Apr. - June
2. The National Archives of the U.K. AIR 1/1946/204/249/2 Operation orders: 54 and 83 Wing. 1918 July - Nov.
3. The National Archives of the U.K. AIR 1/1946/204/249/3 Bomb raid and orders, also Intelligence reports. 1918 July - Aug.
4. The National Archives of the U.K. AIR 1/1946/204/249/4 Bomb raid reports. 1918 Sept. - Nov.
5. The National Archives of the U.K. AIR 1/1946/204/249/6 Recommendations for honours and awards. 1918 July - Nov.
6. The National Archives of the U.K. AIR 76/168/49 Air Ministry and Air Force records
7. The National Archives of the U.K. ADM 273/21/282 A.C.G. Fowler service records
8. The National Archives of the U.K. AIR 76/145/147 C.C. Eaves records
9. The National Archives of the U.K. AIR 76/159/143 J.S. Ferguson records
10. The National Archives of the U.K. AIR 76/136/42 H.R. Dodd records
11. The National Archives of the U.K. AIR 76/156/92 A. Fairhurst records
12. The National Archives of the U.K. AIR 76/255/84 E.C. Jeffkins records
13. The National Archives of the U.K. AIR 76/411/5 T.V. Preedy records
14. The National Archives of the U.K. AIR 1/1997/204/273/204 GoC IF to Air Min Sept 17 1918
15. The National Archives of the U.K. AIR 1/1947/204/295/5 215 Sqn bomb raid report, intelligence summaries 17 Sept 1918
16. The National Archives of the U.K. AIR 1/1649/204/95/9 VIII Brigade RAF 41st and 83rd Wings: Correspondence and reports Casualties Sept 1918-Feb 1919
17. The National Archives of the U.K. AIR 1/1228/204/5/2634 215 combat reports Aug 1918
18. The National Archives of the U.K. AIR 1/1734/204/134/1 1 Jul-31, Dec 1918 83rd wing RAF history data

19. The National Archives of the U.K. AIR 1/184/15/218/1 History of 215 Squadron R.A.F. Late No. 15 R.N.A.S.

20. The National Archives of the U.K. AIR 1/820/204/4/1321 Historic Squadron Documents Combat Reports (1 – 215) 1914-1918

21. The National Archives of the U.K. AIR 1/1949/204/249/4 R.A.F. Bomb Raid Reports 01 Sep – 30 Nov, 1918

22. H.A, Jones, The War in the Air Vol VI: Being the Story of the Part Played in the Great War by the Royal Air Force, The Naval and Military Press Ltd., Uckfield, England and The Imperial War Museum, London, England, 1937

23. H.A, Jones, The War in the Air (Appendices) Being the Story of the Part Played in the Great War by the Royal Air Force, The Naval and Military Press Ltd., Uckfield, England and The Imperial War Museum, London, England, 1937

24. George G. Williams, Biplanes and Bombsights: British Bombing in World War I, Air University Press, US Air Force, Maxwell AFB, USA,1999

25. Rob Langham, 'Bloody Paralyser': The Giant Handley Page Bombers of World War I, Fonthill Media Limited., Stroud, UK, 2016

26. Lieutenant H.B. Monaghan R.F.C., The Big Bombers of World War I, a Canadian's Journal, Ray Gentle/Communications, Ltd., Burlington, Canada

27. C.P.O.Bartlett, Bomber Pilot 1916-1918, Edited by Chaz Bowyer, Ian Allan Ltd., London, U.K., 1974

28. Chaz Bowyer, Handley Page Bombers of World War One, Aston Publications Limited, Bourne End, U.K. 1992

29. Clive Semple, Edited by Wing Commander A. Mawby, Diary of a Night Bomber Pilot in World War I, Spellmount Limited, Stroud, U.K., 2008

30. Paul Bewsher, Green Balls, The Adventures of a Night Bomber, Greenhill Books, 1920

31. Alan Morris, The First of Many: The Story of the Independent Force, RAF, Jarrolds Publishers (London) Ltd., London, U.K., 1968

32. A.R. Kingsford, Night Raiders of the Air, John Hamilton, London 1930

33. C.H. Barnes, Handley Page's 'Bloody Paralyser', Air Enthusiast, Vol 5, No. 2, pp74-81 Trenchard Reports Joint Services Command and Staff College GB 3188 JSCSC IF 2/2:

34. Reports on the Effects and Results of the Bombing of Germany by the 8th Brigade and Independent Force, Royal Air Force Railways

35. Reports on the Effects and Results of the Bombing of Germany by the 8th Brigade and Independent Force, Royal Air Force: Blast Furnaces

36. Department of Intelligence, Reports on the Effects and Results of the Bombing of Germany by the 8th Brigade and Independent Force, Royal Air Force (D) Aerodromes

37. Reports on the Effects and Results of the Bombing of Germany by the 8th Brigade and Independent Force, Royal Air Force: Industrial Centres

38. Department of Air Intelligence, Reports on the Effects and Results of the Bombing of Germany by the 8th Brigade and Independent Force, Royal Air Force (F) Hostile Counter Measures

39. Department of Intelligence, Reports on the Effects and Results of the Bombing of Germany by the 8th Brigade and Independent Force, Royal Air Force Miscellaneous Photographs

40. Reports on the Effects and Results of the Bombing of Germany by the 8th Brigade and Independent Force, Royal Air Force: Bombs

41. Wg Cdr J.E.A. Baldwin, Experiences of Bombing with the Independent Force, 1918, A selection of lectures and essays from the work of the Officers attending the first course at the Royal Air Force Staff College 1922-1923

42. Tenth Supplement to the London Gazette, 1 January, 1919, pages 133-138

43. Flying Fury: Five Years In The Royal Flying Corps [Illustrated Edition], By James Thomas Byford McCudden VC DSO & Bar, MC & Bar MM, Ace Publishing Corporation, 1968

44. "Memorandum on the Tactics to be Adopted in Bombing the Industrial Centres of Germany", 23 June 1918 Trenchard papers, RAF Hendon File 1/10/4

45. "British air policy in the First World War", By Malcolm Cooper, London ; Boston : Allen & Unwin, 1986

46. Report, "Review of Air Situation and Strategy for the Information of the Imperial War Cabinet", by the Chief of the Air Staff, 27 June 1918.

47. "Dispatch on the work of the Independent Force, 5th June to 11th November 1918" by Major-General Sir Hugh Trenchard to Lord Weir, Secretary of State for Air, 12 December 1918.

48. History of the Second World War: by Charles WEBSTER and , CHARLES and Noble FRANKLAND, United Kingdom Military Series; London: H.M.S.O., 1961

49. https://edwardwillett.com/2008/12/the-first-world-war-memoirs-of-sampson-j-goodfellow-part-37-home-to-canada/: accessed 10 May, 2018

Index

175

Notes